English as a Second Language

First Year of Secondary Cycle Two

Philippa Parks
Tanja Vaillancourt

Activity Book

5757, RUE CYPIHOT, SAINT-LAURENT (QUÉBEC) H4S 1R3
TÉLÉPHONE : (514) 334-2690   TÉLÉCOPIEUR : (514) 334-1196
info@erpi.com   www.erpi.com

Managing editor
Sharnee Chait

Project editor
Lee Ann Balazuc

Proofreader
My-Trang Nguyen

Photo research
Pierre-Richard Bernier

Art director
Hélène Cousineau

Graphic design coordinator
François Lambert

Graphic design and layout
Accent tonique

Illustrations
Frédérick Fontaine
Jean-François Vachon

© ÉDITIONS DU RENOUVEAU PÉDAGOGIQUE INC., 2007

Tous droits réservés.
On ne peut reproduire aucun extrait de ce livre sous quelque forme ou par quelque procédé que ce soit – sur machine électronique, mécanique, à photocopier ou à enregistrer, ou autrement – sans avoir obtenu au préalable la permission écrite des ÉDITIONS DU RENOUVEAU PÉDAGOGIQUE INC.

All rights reserved. No part of this publication may be reproduced, stored in a retrieval system, or transmitted in any form or by any means, electronic, mechanical, photocopying, recording, or otherwise without the prior written permission of ÉDITIONS DU RENOUVEAU PÉDAGOGIQUE INC.

Registration of copyright – Bibliothèque et Archives nationales du Québec, 2007
Registration of copyright – Library and Archives Canada, 2007

Printed in Canada   123456789 SO 0987
ISBN 978-2-7613-2283-6   10833 ABCD OF10

Photo Credits

ASSOCIATED PRESS:
p. 22 (bottom)

CORBIS:
p. 22: G. Palmer (top); p. 28: P. Turnley; p. 33: J. Madere; p. 41: G. D. Landsman; p. 51: T. Khan (top); p. 53: Sunset Boulevard (top left); p. 53: D. G. Houser (top middle right); p. 59: H. Winkler/A. B./zefa; p. 80: Atlantide Travel; p. 85: P. Chevreuil; p. 87: D. M. Curtin/zefa; p. 93: P. Robert/Sygma; p. 97: S. Marcus; p. 100: D. Bartuff

CP IMAGES:
p. 53 (top left middle and top right); p. 54; p. 56; p. 58; p. 65; p. 90; p. 94; p. 95

GETTY IMAGES:
p. 1: B. Erlinger

ISTOCKPHOTO:
p. 5: B. Evers; p. 7; p. 15: K. Cline; p. 51 (bottom); p. 67; p. 70: C. Waldegger; p. 78: G. Andrushko; p. 89; p.102

LIAM DANIEL:
p.11

PHOTOTHÈQUE ERPI:
p.2; p. 9; p. 21; p. 31; p. 36; p. 37; p. 39; p. 43; p. 45; p. 57; p. 77; p.101

SHUTTERSTOCK:
p. 29

Table of Contents

Unit 1 Travel the World in English 1
Smart Structures: Questions, Simple Present Tense

Unit 2 Change the Music, Change the Mood 11
Smart Structure: Simple Past Tense

Unit 3 Change My World, Change Our World 21
Smart Structure: Pronouns and Possessive Adjectives

Unit 4 Websites and E-mail: Use Your Judgment 31
Smart Structure: Articles

Unit 5 How Much Is Too Much? 41
Smart Structure: Modals and Conditional Form

Review 1 51

Unit 6 Are You Game to Learn? 57
Smart Structure: Present Progressive Tense

Unit 7 Extreme Sports and Advertising 67
Smart Structure: Comparatives and Superlatives

Unit 8 I'm a Survivor 77
Smart Structure: Prepositions

Unit 9 Fear in the News 87
Smart Structure: Past Progressive Tense

Unit 10 Strange and Unusual Jobs 97
Smart Structure: Future Tense

Review 2 107

Irregular Verbs 113
Spelling Log 115
Grammar Log 116

Dear students and teachers,

If someone asked us to name something that changed our lives, we would both say, "Learning a second language!"

We come from different backgrounds. Tanja grew up in Germany and moved to Québec as a teenager where she learned English as a second language. Philippa grew up in Ontario where she studied French. We know how learning another language can change your life. It opens up opportunities to meet new friends, learn about new people, travel and even find employment in other cities, provinces and countries. Learning another language allows you to watch movies in their original language, read new books, and understand the words to your favourite songs. Learning English inspired Tanja to become an English teacher. Learning French inspired Philippa to move to Québec and eventually marry a French Québecois!

Coming together to work on this book was an inspiring moment for both of us. It gave us the opportunity to transmit our passion for learning second languages to you. We hope that this book inspires you too!

Philippa Parks

Tanja Vaillancourt

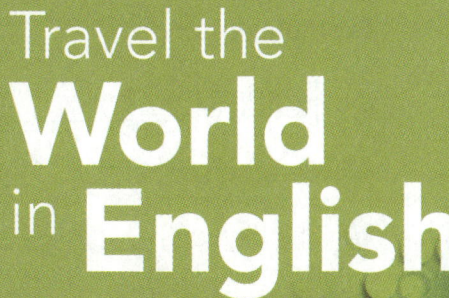

Travel the World in English

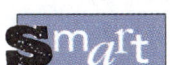

Structure
Questions

Question Word	Refers to	Example
Who?	a person	**Who** speaks English?
What?	an object, a thing, a name	**What** city do you want to visit?
Where?	a place	**Where** do you live?
When?	a time or a date	**When** were you born?
Why?	a reason	**Why** do you like to speak English?
Whose?	a belonging	**Whose** father speaks English?
Which?	a distinction	**Which** city do you prefer?
How?	a way, a manner	**How** are you today?

How can be used together with many adjectives:
How far? *How* big? *How* long? *How* interesting? *How* many?

How many is used for things you can count (friends, desks, people):
How many classmates watch English programs on TV?
How many video games do you have?

How much is used for things you can't count (sugar, coffee, money):
How much English do you speak?
How much money do you have?

Name: _____ Group: _____ Date: _____

1 The Right Question Word

› Find the correct question word that goes with the answer given.

Example: In London _____Where_____

1. Next week _____
2. Because I am happy _____
3. The blue one _____
4. 55 cm _____
5. My friend Nadine _____
6. At the CN Tower _____
7. Two hamburgers _____
8. Money _____
9. It's mine _____
10. A chair _____

2 An Interview

› Find the right question word and write it in the first blank space for each question.
› Then interview your partner to get to know him or her better, using these questions.
› Write your partner's answers in the spaces after the questions.

Example: _____How_____ are you? _____I am fine._____

1. _____ is your name? _____
2. _____ old are you? _____
3. _____ is your birthday? _____
4. _____ is your star sign? _____
5. _____ do you live? _____
6. _____ brothers and sisters do you have? _____
7. _____ are your parents' names? _____
8. _____ do you get home from school? _____
9. _____ do you go to bed? _____
10. _____ do you speak English? _____

Unit 1 | Travel the World in English

Structure

Questions

Information Questions		
There are two ways to form information questions using question words:		
question word	**verb "to be"**	**rest of question**
What	are	coins?
Where	is	Australia?

question word	**auxiliary**	**subject**	**verb**	**rest of question**
Where	do	you	want	to travel?
Why	does	the teacher	speak	so quickly?

Yes/No Questions				
There are two ways to form yes/no questions:				
verb "to be"	**subject**	**adjective**	**answer**	
Are	you	bilingual?	Yes, I am.	
Is	your mother	American?	No, she isn't.	

auxiliary	**subject**	**verb**	**rest of question**	**answer**
Do	you	understand	Chinese?	Not really.
Does	she	speak	Greek?	Yes, she does.

3 Which Answer Is Correct?

> Circle the letter of the response that correctly answers each question.

Example:

What's his name?
a) My name is John.
b) Your name is Penelope.
c) His name is Harry.
d) I like his name.

1 Where do you live?
a) I often visit Québec.
b) I want to live in Sherbrooke.
c) I live in Trois-Rivières.
d) You live in Coaticook.

2 What do you wear to school?
a) I like jeans.
b) I wear a uniform.
c) She wears a uniform.
d) I am wearing jeans and a T-shirt.

3 Do you study in your room?
a) Yes, I dance all the time.
b) No, I study in the basement.
c) Yes, tomorrow.
d) Yes, on Friday.

4 What time is it?
a) It's morning.
b) It's too late.
c) It's Saturday.
d) It's two minutes to two.

5 How old is your mother?
a) She is 37.
b) She has 37.
c) She have 37.
d) She is young.

Express Yourself Activity Book | Unit 1 | 3

Name: _____ Group: _____ Date: _____

4 Writing Information Questions

> Form a question with the following sentences by replacing the underlined word or phrase with a question word.

Example: Paul goes <u>to a concert</u> every week.
Where does Paul go every week?

❶ Juan studies at the library <u>every Wednesday</u>.
_____

❷ I eat <u>five cookies</u> after supper.
_____

❸ I like the binder <u>with the pink flowers on it</u>.
_____

❹ I am always ready to leave <u>at 7:00</u> in the morning.
_____

❺ We celebrate Christmas <u>in England</u> every year.
_____

5 Different Words, Different Countries

If you visit England, you will find that they have different words than we do in Canada for certain things. Sometimes they even use the same words but mean something completely different!

> Look at the Canadian words and their British equivalents.
> Change the verb from the infinitive to the simple present tense (see Smart Structure, pages 5–6).
> Then match the Canadian word to its British equivalent.

Canada	Britain
Example:	
❶ We (to eat) _eat_ **chips** and drink soda. _a_	a) She (to enjoy) _enjoys_ **crisps**.
❷ She (to drive) _____ a big **truck**. ___	b) Sarah (to order) _____ **chips** with her fish.
❸ The **trunks** of these cars (to be) _____ full. ___	c) Jerry (to own) _____ a **lorry**.
❹ I (to knit) _____ **sweaters**. ___	d) We (to wear) _____ **jumpers**.
❺ He (to prefer) _____ his **fries** with ketchup. ___	e) The **boot** of my car (to have) _____ a dent in it!

4 Unit 1 | Travel the World in English

Name: _____ Group: _____ Date: _____

6 Smart Words Review

You learned new words in this first unit. Do you remember what they were?

> Unscramble each of the smart words.

Example: s e i t i i l c a f   facilities

1. i r u l n g h   _____
2. s e n t r d   _____
3. t n e c s e d   _____
4. h b r a o u r   _____
5. a a o d b r   _____
6. y b g r u   _____
7. r r f e y   _____
8. l o p o   _____
9. d r a c p o s t   _____
10. e r k c t c i   _____

Structure

Simple Present Tense

Verb "To Be"		
Negative form: Add **not**.		
Question form: Verb is placed before the subject.		
Affirmative (contraction)	**Negative** (contraction)	**Question**
I **am** (I'm)	I **am not** (I'm not)	**Am** I in the right room?
You **are** (you're)	You **are not** (you're not)	**Are** you / we / they bilingual?
He **is** / she **is** / it **is** (he's / she's / it's)	He **is not** (he's not / he isn't)	**Is** he Australian?
We **are** (we're)	We / They **are not** (we're not / they aren't)	
They **are** (they're)		

Express Yourself Activity Book | Unit 1 | 5

Name: _____ Group: _____ Date: _____

Regular Verbs
Add **s** for third person singular. Add **es** for words ending in sh, ch, s, x and o. **Negative form:** Add **do not** or **does not** before the verb. **Question form:** Start the question with **do** or **does**. **Exception:** Verb "to have" He / she / it **has**

Affirmative	Negative (contraction)	Question
I **sing** You **talk** He / she / it **sings** / **washes** We **love** They **need**	I **do not** sing. (don't) You **do not** sing. (don't) He **does not** sing. (doesn't) We **do not** sing. (don't) They **do not** sing. (don't)	**Do** I **need** anything? **Do** you / we / they **sing**? **Does** he / she / it **need** something?

7 Verb Contractions

> Complete each sentence with the simple present verb "to be" in both its long form and its contraction form.

> Use the subject in parentheses to complete each sentence.

Affirmative

Example: ___You are / You're___ a wonderful guy. (You)

1. _____ fourteen years old. (I)
2. _____ shy. (She)
3. _____ blue. (It)
4. _____ the neighbours. (We)
5. _____ funny. (You)

Negative

Example: ___You are not / You aren't___ a terrible guy. (You)

6. _____ thirteen years old. (I)
7. _____ the teacher. (He)
8. _____ outgoing. (She)
9. _____ funny. (You)
10. _____ bilingual. (They)

Unit 1 | Travel the World in English

Name: _____ Group: _____ Date: _____

8 An Australian Beach

Australia is famous for its beaches.

› Answer the questions about what you see in this beach scene.

Example: Is the sunshine bright? *Yes, the sunshine is bright.*

1. Is the dog active? _____
2. Is the picnic basket small? _____
3. Are the children happy? _____
4. Is the water safe? _____
5. Are the people hungry? _____

9 Key Words

› Identify the key words that we use with the simple present by placing a check mark beside them.

Example: all the time ✓

1. yesterday ☐
2. tomorrow ☐
3. sometimes ☐
4. every day ☐
5. next week ☐
6. three hours ago ☐
7. often ☐
8. usually ☐

Express Yourself Activity Book | Unit 1 7

Name: _____ Group: _____ Date: _____

10 How I Learned English

This text is about Marco, a Costa Rican man who explains how he learned English. He gives tips on what helped him to learn so that he could travel the world in English.

What is the best way to learn English? Read this text to find out what the author suggests!

> Read the following text. See page 9 for the Smart Words definitions in the text.

My name is Marco Brenes. I live in Costa Rica and my mother tongue is Spanish. I am a professional **diver** and I go to many international competitions. I am also an enthusiastic learner of English.

I had my first real contact with English when I was six years old. My dad inspired me to listen to English music when we were driving in his car. I started listening to his CDs and I remember that at the beginning I did not understand anything. Soon, by listening to the songs **over and over** again, I started to understand individual words, like the ones that appeared in the titles of songs. Then I learned to sing the songs by heart.

At first English was really difficult. In secondary school, I remember my English teacher saying, "Marco, you make so many mistakes, your pronunciation is not clear and you speak so slowly … I can see you love English but you have to practise more …." I was discouraged.

Then one day, my friend gave me a video game in English—it was fun and I learned new English words.

My mother started to buy me English comic books to read. The pictures helped me to understand the story. I started reading books without pictures in English too. I discovered that it is easier to understand the book in English if you read it in your own language first.

Today, I can understand everything and speaking English gives me a lot of pleasure. I feel so **proud** when I meet people from all around the world and speak English. Everybody learns English so that people from every nationality can communicate together. It is a universal language. I really love the language and the fun things it **allows** me to do: watch American action movies, read comics and surf the web.

Here are my tips to help you learn:

1. Watch a lot of English TV.
2. Speak English five minutes every day with your best friend just to get some practice.
3. Read about things that interest you.
4. Write in English as often as you can. Today, with the Internet, it is so easy to do.

Good luck!

> Answer these questions.

1. What nationality is Marco? _____

2. How did his dad inspire him to learn English? _____
_____

Name: _____ Group: _____ Date: _____

3 Why did Marco read the books in his own language first? _____
_____

4 Name five fun things he can do in English now. _____
_____

5 Which sentence proves that it was difficult for Marco to learn English?
_____
_____

6 Name three tips Marco suggests for learning English.
_____
_____
_____

7 Which tip will you try? _____
_____

Smart Words

diver = an athlete who plunges into water

over and over = many times

proud = happy because of what you accomplish

allows = permits

11 Affirmative, Negative and Question Form

> Transform these sentences to the affirmative form, the negative form and the question form.

Example: He (to live) on this street.
He lives on this street.
He does not (doesn't) live on this street.
Does he live on this street?

1 She (to speak) English very well.
_____
_____
_____

2 They (to travel) to London every year.
_____
_____
_____

3 We (to go) to school during the week.
_____
_____
_____

Express Yourself Activity Book | Unit 1 | 9

Name: _____ Group: _____ Date: _____

Strategy

12 Substitute

When you don't remember how to say a word, you can say it in another way.

> How could you explain or rephrase these words?
> Write your own definition of each word.
> Then ask your partner to guess what the word is, using your definition.

Example: television You watch shows on it. It is usually in the living room.

1. language _____
2. swimming _____
3. stamp _____
4. England _____
5. Statue of Liberty _____
6. postcard _____
7. polo _____
8. harbour _____

13 A Cartoon Caption

This cartoon is related to the theme of the unit.

> Write a caption for the cartoon.
> Make your caption funny or original!

10 | Unit 1 | Travel the World in English

Unit 2

Change the Music, Change the Mood

Structure

Simple Past Tense

Regular Verbs		
Add **ed** at the end of the verb. **Negative form:** Add **did not** before the verb. You can also use the contraction **didn't**. **Question form:** Add **did** before the subject.		
Affirmative	**Negative** (contraction)	**Question**
I **watched** the movie. You **listened** to the music. She **worked** hard. We **liked** the film. They **studied** at the library.	I **did not watch** the movie. (didn't) You **did not listen** to the music. (didn't) He **did not work** hard. (didn't) We **did not like** the film. (didn't) They **did not study** at the library. (didn't)	**Did** I **watch** the movie? **Did** you **listen** to the music? **Did** he/she **work** hard? **Did** we **like** the film? **Did** they **study** at the library?

Express Yourself Activity Book | Unit 2 | 11

Name: _____ Group: _____ Date: _____

1 A Movie Scene

When was the last time you watched a movie? What was it about? Was it a good film? Why?

If you want to talk about movies that you have seen, you will need to use the simple past tense.

> Look at the picture below.
> Unscramble the sentences to find out what happened in this scene.
> Change the verbs into the simple past.

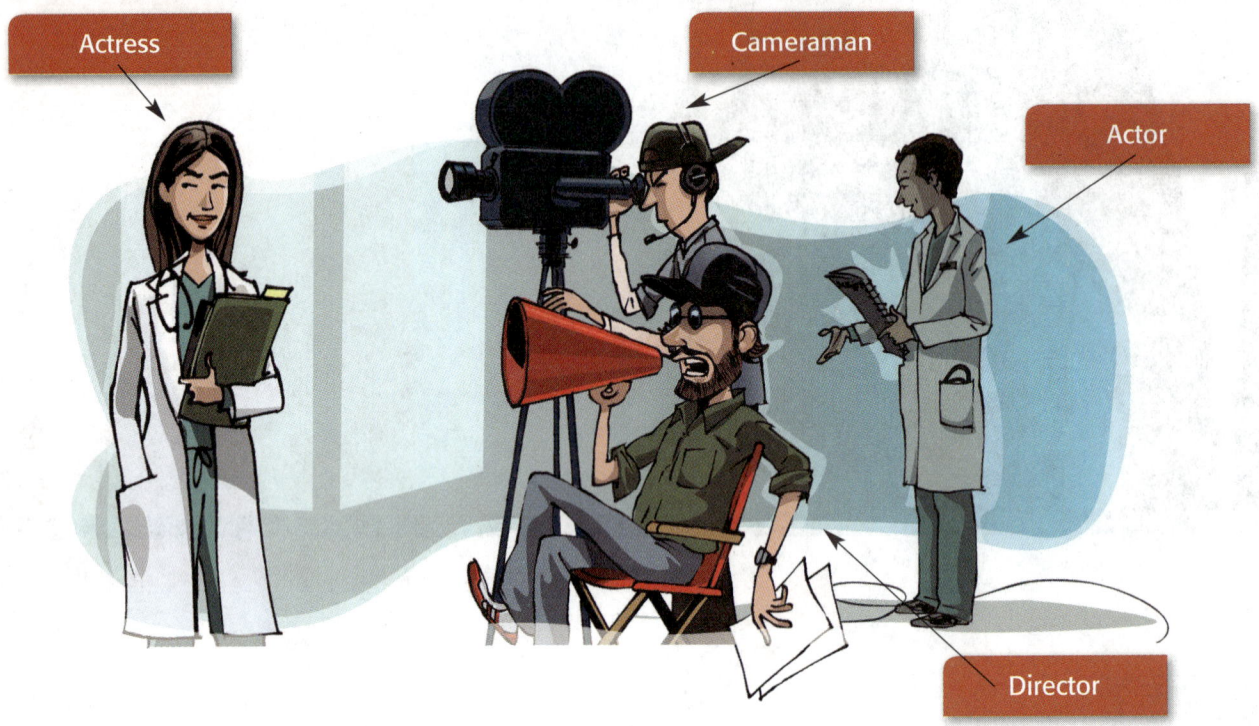

Example: read / lines / her / actress / the

The actress read her lines.

① **shout** / the / actors / the / director / at

_____

② **practise** / an / actor / lines / his

_____

③ **film** / the / cameraman / the / scene

_____

④ **look** / her / script / the / actress / at

_____

⑤ **ask** / a / question / the / director / the / actor

_____

12 Unit 2 | Change the Music, Change the Mood

Name: _____ Group: _____ Date: _____

2 Interview Notes

Poor Bob (the film critic) can't find his extra notes from his last interview with Tom Crade! He has some notes that he took, but he needs the questions and answers. Help him remember what he asked Tom Crade and what the answers were.

> First, read the notes.
> Second, write a question using the simple past tense and "you."
> Third, write the answer to the question in a complete sentence.

Example: Act in any horror movies? (Yes, three)

   Q: Did you act in any horror movies?
   A: Yes, I acted in three horror movies.

❶ Ever help another actor? (Yes, Nikki Kipman, ex-wife)

   Q: _____
   A: _____

❷ Ever sing a song in a film? (No)

   Q: _____
   A: _____

❸ Ever think about changing careers? (Yes)

   Q: _____
   A: _____

❹ Want to be a director? (Yes)

   Q: _____
   A: _____

❺ Ever cry in a movie? (No, never)

   Q: _____
   A: _____

❻ Learn anything important about acting? (No)

   Q: _____
   A: _____

❼ Ever do your own stunts? (No, never)

   Q: _____
   A: _____

Name: _____ Group: _____ Date: _____

Structure

Simple Past Tense

Verb "To Be"		
Affirmative	**Negative** (contraction)	**Question**
I **was**	I **was not** (wasn't)	**Was** I?
You **were**	You **were not** (weren't)	**Were** you?
She / he / it **was**	She / he / it **was not** (wasn't)	**Was** she / he / it?
We **were**	We **were not** (weren't)	**Were** we?
You **were**	You **were not** (weren't)	**Were** you?
They **were**	They **were not** (weren't)	**Were** they?

3 An Interview

The world-famous film star, Tom Crade, is retiring. Film critics Betty and Bob are looking back at their last interview with Tom Crade.

› Read the interview.
› Change the "to be" verbs from the simple present to the simple past.
› Practise saying the new interview with a partner.

Betty: Our guest on the show (is) _was_ Mr. Tom Crade. Tom (is) _____ a star in many blockbuster films. He (is) _____ famous for his acting—especially in action films. He and his ex-wife, Nikki Kipman, (are) _____ in a new movie called *The UnDead*.

Bob: (Are) _____ you nervous about the film, Tom?

Tom: Bob, I (am) _____ a great actor. I (am) _____ never nervous.

Betty: What about your new wife, Kitty Halms? (Is) _____ she jealous?

Tom: Kitty (is) _____ never jealous. We (are) _____ a great team. She (is) _____ very supportive.

Bob: (Are) _____ Kitty and Nikki popular with your fans?

Tom: My fans (are) _____ crazy about Nikki and Kitty, but of course, I (am) _____ their hero. They (are) _____ excited to see me in any film.

Betty: (Are) _____ there any problems acting with your ex-wife?

Tom: None, Betty. I (am) _____ a great actor and Nikki (is) _____ not too bad, either.

14 Unit 2 | Change the Music, Change the Mood

Name: _____ Group: _____ Date: _____

s^ma^rt Structure

Simple Past Tense

Irregular Verbs

Use your irregular verb list (page 113).

Affirmative	Negative (contraction)	Question
I **began** to write.	I **did not begin** to write. (didn't)	**Did** you **begin** to write?
You **felt** happy.	You **did not feel** happy. (didn't)	**Did** you **feel** happy?
He **heard** the music.	She **did not hear** the music. (didn't)	**Did** he/she **hear** the music?
We **ate** lunch.	We **did not eat**. (didn't)	**Did** we **eat**?
They **had** a discussion.	They **did not have** a discussion. (didn't)	**Did** they **have** a discussion?

4 Silent Movies

› Underline the correct past-tense verb form in the questions and answers and learn about what cinema was like without sound.

Example:

Q: (Do they eat / Do they eated / Did they eat) popcorn at the movies?

A: Yes, they (eat / eated / ate) popcorn and many other snacks!

① Q: (Did they have / Do they have / Did they had) many famous actors?

A: In the days before movies had sound, we (seen / seed / saw) many famous actors like Charlie Chaplin, Mary Pickford and Buster Keaton.

② Q: (Do they heard / Did they heard / Did they hear) the dialogue?

A: People (do not hear / did not hear / do not heared) the actors, because the actors (did not speak / do not speak / did not spoke).

③ Q: How much (do it cost / did it cost / did it costed) to go to the movies?

A: A movie ticket (cost / costed / cast) ten cents.

④ Q: Who (go / gone / went) to the movies?

A: Everyone (do / done / did)! Men (bringed / brang / brought) women to the cinema and even (paid / payed / payt) for their tickets!

⑤ Q: Why (do they went / did they go / did they went) to the movies?

A: Many people (thought / think / thinked) that the cinema (is / was / were) the best way to relax.

Express Yourself Activity Book | Unit 2 | 15

5 A Movie Review

> Read the following text.
> Fill in the blanks with these words from your Unit 2 Smart Words Review.
> Then circle all the verbs from this paragraph that are in the past tense.

cameo	awesome	heart	happy	tale
scared	acting	forum post	expecting	nostalgia

Yesterday, I (watched) a film. My friend told me that the film was _awesome_ so I went to the video store and rented it. When I watched it, I felt very _____ because it was a horror film. The director used the music as a tool to touch my _____. The music was pretty good. The _____ in the film was not very good. The actors did not tell the _____ very well. I was _____ better acting—especially from Tom Crade, who had a _____ in the film. I was _____ when the film was over. It was so bad that I decided to write what I thought about the movie on a _____ on the Internet. After I watched this movie, I felt _____ for the horror films I saw when I was a little kid. They were really scary!

> Write the past-tense verbs on the lines below (write each verb only once).
> Write the base form of the verb next to the past-tense form.

Example: watched / to watch

1. _____
2. _____
3. _____
4. _____
5. _____
6. _____
7. _____
8. _____
9. _____
10. _____

16 Unit 2 | Change the Music, Change the Mood

Name: _____ Group: _____ Date: _____

6 A Film Crossword Puzzle

What new words did you learn in this unit?

> Test what you know by filling in this crossword puzzle. Some of the words are Smart Words, while others appear throughout the unit.

> Use the clues below to help you find these words.

actors   impact   scene
blockbuster   mood   script
critic   nostalgia   shortcut
film   rate   soundtrack
host   review   cameo

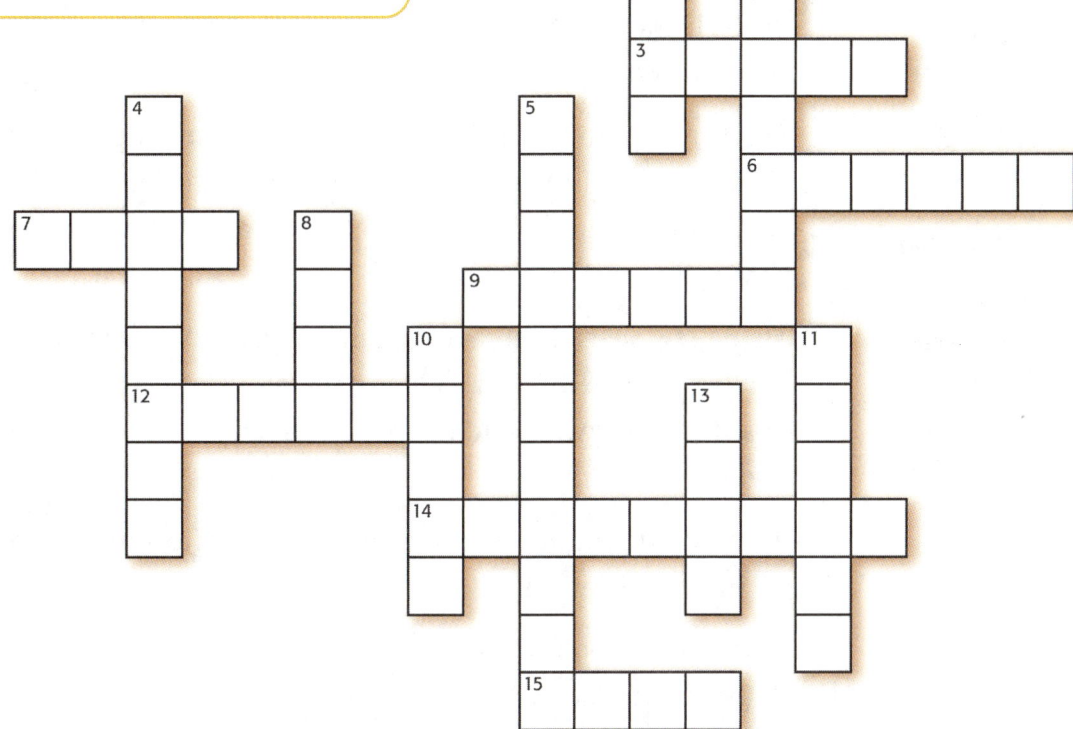

Across

3 short appearance in a movie by a famous person
6 people who play a part in a film
7 emotion
9 the written form of a play or film
12 person who writes movie reviews for a living
14 feeling sentimental about old times
15 to give a mark (usually on ten)

Down

1 the sounds and music in a film
2 to have an important effect
4 quick way to get somewhere without effort
5 film that is a huge success
8 someone who introduces guests on a show
10 short part of a movie
11 someone's impression of a movie
13 another word for a movie

Express Yourself Activity Book | Unit 2 | 17

Name: _____ Group: _____ Date: _____

7 Hollywood History

Most English-language films in the world are made in Hollywood, California. How much do you know about Hollywood's history?

> Read this text about Hollywood's history.
> Use the Smart Words to help you understand it.
> Underline all the past-tense verbs in the text.

Smart Words

explorer = someone who travels to places that people have not visited before

grain = the seeds of crops such as corn, wheat, etc.

pineapple = a tropical fruit

sprang up (spring up) = to suddenly appear or exist

built (to build) = to construct

film set = place where movies are filmed

Hollywood History

When Spanish **explorers** came to California, the only inhabitants were Native Americans. By the 1870s, there were many farms in the area. People grew **grain**, bananas and **pineapples**.

In 1911, the Nestor Company opened Hollywood's first film studio in an old tavern.

Banks, restaurants, clubs and movie palaces **sprang up** in the 1920s and 1930s. People also built many houses and apartments on Hollywood Boulevard for the enormous numbers of people who worked on the **film sets**.

After a few years, Hollywood changed again. Many movie stars decided to move to Beverly Hills. When they moved, the stores and restaurants closed in Hollywood and opened in Beverly Hills to be closer to their clients.

In the 1960s, music recording studios and offices moved to Hollywood on Sunset Boulevard.

Today, Hollywood is a diverse, vital and active community. In 1985, Hollywood officially became an Historic Place.

18 · Unit 2 | Change the Music, Change the Mood

Name: _____ Group: _____ Date: _____

8 True or False

> Decide whether the following statements are true or false.

> Put a check mark in the appropriate column for each statement.

		True:	False:
1	The first inhabitants of Hollywood were the Spanish.		
2	Hollywood started as a farming community in the 1870s.		
3	People grew pineapples and kiwis in Hollywood.		
4	The first film studio opened in 1950.		
5	The first film studio was built in an old tavern.		
6	Movie stars moved from Beverly Hills to Hollywood.		
7	In the 1920s, Hollywood was filled with gangsters.		
8	Many people worked in Hollywood on the film sets.		
9	People built movie theatres, restaurants and apartments along Hollywood Boulevard.		
10	Hollywood became an Historic Place in 1985.		

9 When Did It Happen?

> Write the events that happened in Hollywood next to the dates in the timeline below:

Before 1870 Hollywood was discovered by the Spanish.

1870s _____

1911 _____

1920s _____

1960s _____

1985 _____

Express Yourself Activity Book | Unit 2 | 19

Name: _____ Group: _____ Date: _____

Strategy

10 Semantic Mapping

Use semantic mapping to help you organize your thoughts, ideas and information so that they are clearer to you.

› Make a semantic map for the last movie you watched.
› Add in these ideas/questions:

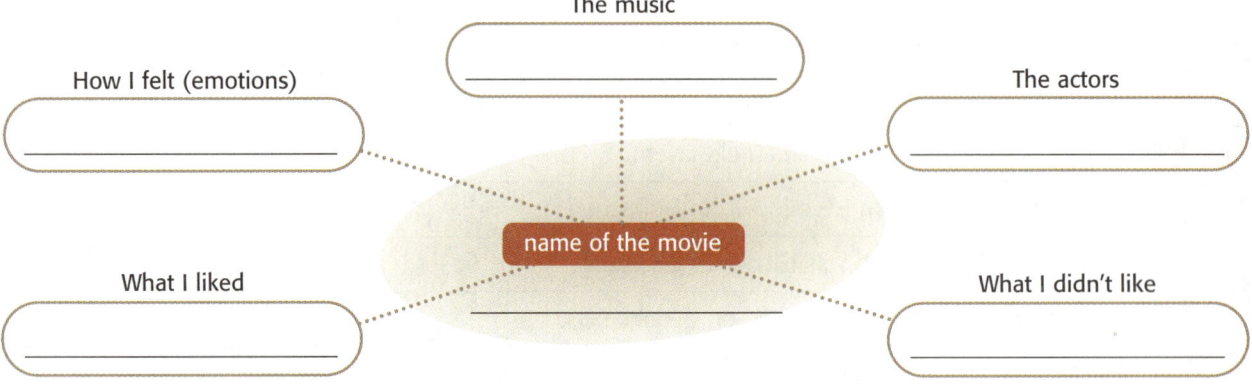

› When you are finished, ask your partner to guess the movie title from the clues you wrote.

11 A Cartoon Caption

This cartoon is related to the theme of the unit.

› Write a caption for the cartoon.
› Make your caption funny or original!

Unit 2 | Change the Music, Change the Mood

Unit 3

Change **My** World, Change **Our** World

Structure

Pronouns and Possessive Adjectives

Subject Pronoun	Object Pronoun	Reflexive Pronoun	Possessive Pronoun	Possessive Adjective
Acts as the subject	Acts as an object	Refers to the subject	Acts as a marker of possession and defines ownership	Indicates ownership
I You He, she, it We You They	Me You Him, her, it Us You Them	Myself Yourself Himself, herself, itself Ourselves Yourselves Themselves	Mine Yours His, hers Ours Yours Theirs	My Your His, her, its Our Your Their
She saved my life.	She saved **me**.	He repaired it **himself**.	The book is **yours**.	It is **her** medal.

Express Yourself Activity Book | Unit 3 | 21

Name: _____ Group: _____ Date: _____

1 Subject Pronouns

> Choose the correct subject pronoun.
> Use the words in parentheses to help you.

Example: ___She___ wants to go to Africa.
(My best friend)

1. _____ always visits his grandparents.
(Willy)

2. _____ is happy.
(The teacher)

3. _____ are on the wall.
(The love poems)

4. _____ jumped up and down.
(The winner of the contest)

5. _____ do volunteer work every weekend.
(My mother and I)

6. _____ prepares supper every night.
(Charles-Alexandre)

7. _____ help our brothers and sisters.
(My friends and I)

8. _____ inspire me.
(Your parents)

2 Object Pronouns

Which pronoun should replace the underlined phrase in the sentence?

> Circle the correct answer.

Example: Gilbert will give Philippa a big kiss. (him / it /(her))

1. The teacher always gives the students (me / them / you) homework.

2. I read the book to my little sister. (her / us / him)

3. The boys are getting pink flowers for their girlfriends. (it / them / her)

4. My father is writing a love letter to my mom. (him / her / me)

5. I don't know how to help my brother. (she / him / it)

6. Open your heart. (it / them / us)

7. Sam is going to visit Annie-Claude. (her / him / me)

8. Can you help these people cross the street, please? (you / us / them)

22 Unit 3 | Change My World, Change Our World

Name: _____ Group: _____ Date: _____

3 Reflexive Pronouns

> Write the correct pronoun in the blank.
> Use the subject in each sentence to help you.
> Check the Smart Structure on page 21 for additional help.

Example: I built the house _____myself._____

1. Valérie came up with this surprise present _____.
2. They took a beautiful photo of _____.
3. Andrew made a birthday card _____.
4. Carolina and Alyssa, did you draw this picture all by _____?
5. We helped _____ to some lemonade at the party.
6. I wrote this interesting article _____.
7. He hurt _____ when he was helping his dad in the yard.
8. Patricia, did you repair the bike _____?
9. If we paint the room _____, it will be much nicer.
10. It's always better if you do it _____.

4 Possessive Pronouns

> Fill in the blank with the correct possessive pronoun.
> Use the objects in the first sentence to help you.

Example: It belongs to Maika. It's ___hers.___

1. It belongs to my father. It's _____.
2. It belongs to her. It's _____.
3. It belongs to Mr. and Mrs. Smith. It's _____.
4. It belongs to me and my wife. It's _____.
5. It belongs to him. It's _____.
6. It belongs to you. It's _____.
7. This is my pen. It's _____.
8. That is your book. It's _____.

Express Yourself Activity Book | Unit 3 | 23

Name: _____ Group: _____ Date: _____

5 Pronouns and Adjectives

› Underline all the pronouns and adjectives you find and identify what kind of pronouns or adjectives they are.

› The first one has been done for you as an example.

possessive adjective

My mother is a wonderful person. She takes care of her family and she also takes care of people in a hospital. Her best quality is her sense of humour. Her coworkers and her patients always talk about how fun she is to have around. You would be surprised by all the funny stories she tells them to make them laugh. We always have a good laugh with her. What is your mom's best quality?

6 The Imperative

The imperative is very easy to use in English:
- Write the base form of the verb.
- Do not write a pronoun before the verb.
- Do not write "to" before the verb.

The following verbs show easy ways to be kind.

> to say   to visit   to forgive   to share   to lend   to be   to offer   to let   ~~to write~~

› Find the right verb for each act of kindness and write it in the imperative form.

Example: _____Write_____ a thank-you note.

❶ _____ mistakes.
❷ _____ a hand.
❸ _____ tolerant.
❹ _____ a hug.
❺ _____ hello.
❻ _____ a smile.
❼ _____ a friend.
❽ _____ another person go first.

24 | Unit 3 | Change My World, Change Our World

Name: _____ Group: _____ Date: _____

7 Unscramble the Story

This is a simple story about kindness.

> Read each sentence and decide where it belongs in the story.
> Put a number in front of each sentence (1–6) to show its order in the story.

___ Jean-Philippe was happy and surprised that his friend came to visit him, and realized that he was a very good friend!

___ Sébastien wondered where his best friend was and called him when he got home from school.

___ After the phone call, he decided to bring Jean-Philippe a video game and his homework.

___ Jean-Philippe had a very bad cold and didn't go to school.

___ He talked to Jean-Philippe's mom, who told him that he had spent the day in bed and was coughing too much to go to school the next day.

___ So that night, Sébastien went over to visit his friend and brought two video games and the homework Jean-Philippe missed.

8 Understanding Vocabulary

> Read each text.
> Fill in the blanks with the Smart Words below.

greeted	highway	hug	injured	injuries
parking meter	~~placemats~~	quarter	random	reward
robbery	volunteer work	wallet	seatbelt	

Example: My mother wants us to use ___placemats___ all the time when we eat at the kitchen table.

❶ I received a _____ for helping to stop a _____.

❷ Every month, I help elderly people in a home doing _____.

❸ Sometimes I put an extra _____ in the _____ for the next person.

❹ People drive too fast on the _____ and get _____ in car accidents.

❺ I _____ my grandmother with a _____ at the front door.

❻ A _____ act of kindness can be as simple as smiling at someone who looks sad.

❼ The woman stopped the thief from stealing the old man's _____.

❽ If you wear your _____, you can avoid _____ if you are in an accident.

Express Yourself Activity Book | Unit 3 | 25

Name: _____ Group: _____ Date: _____

9 Big Brothers Reading

One easy way to change the world is to do volunteer work.

> Before you read the text, read the questions that follow so you will know what information you need to look for as you read.

> While you read the text, use a highlighter to underline all the words you understand. You will notice that there are more words you understand than words you don't understand.

> After reading the text, answer the questions.

Do you know about the Big Brothers program?

The Big Brothers movement started in the United States. A group of men were concerned about young boys in single-parent families who were getting into trouble. In 1903, they decided to help those children by pairing them with a volunteer adult. With a "Big Brother," the boys could have someone to give them friendship, trust and encouragement.

The Big Brothers recognized that caring adults could help many of these kids stay out of trouble, and they set out to find volunteers. By 1916, Big Brothers had spread to 96 cities across the country.

The Big Brothers Association of Canada was founded in 1964. The Association now includes 175 agencies across the country, about 20 of those in Québec.

The Big Brothers Association of Montréal started in 1975. The Big Sisters program was added in 1980. In the same year, the Big Brothers/Big Sisters organization became affiliated with Centraide.

Since it started, the Big Brothers/Big Sisters Association of Montréal has matched more than 4000 children to Big Brothers and Big Sisters. Most of the children come from single-parent families. The youngsters come from various and different backgrounds, all with the common desire to meet a Big Brother or a Big Sister.

Youths who have a Big Brother or Big Sister have a 20 percent higher-than-average high-school graduating rate. Mentor relationships help improve a youngster's self-esteem and create a higher level of confidence.

The Big Brothers organization operates in 35 countries around the world!

Unit 3 | Change My World, Change Our World

Name: _____ Group: _____ Date: _____

> Answer these questions about the text you read:

1 Where and when did this program start?
_____
_____

2 When did the program begin in Québec?
_____
_____

3 How many countries have Big Brothers programs?
_____
_____

4 How many children have been helped?
_____
_____

5 How does the Big Brothers organization help children?
_____
_____

6 What strategy did you use to help yourself understand the text? Did you reread the text? Did you highlight the important words? Did you check in the dictionary?
_____
_____

7 Do you know someone who is a Big Brother?
_____
_____

8 What do you think about this program? Would you like to spend time with an adult mentor?
_____
_____

Express Yourself Activity Book | Unit 3 | 27

Name: _____ Group: _____ Date: _____

10 A Chain of Kindness

Doing something nice starts with something small but can become something big. That's why the title of this unit is "Change My World, Change Our World." The "Pay It Forward" movement showed people that it takes only a small action to change the world.

> Write a chain of kindness using ten sentences that describe acts of kindness.
> Your sentences should go from a small action to a big action.
> Write them with a pencil (not a pen) so you can make changes and play around with the possibilities.

Example:

1. I smiled at someone who looked sad on the bus.
2. That sad person felt better and …
10. … finally, the United Nations decided to help stop the war.

1. _____
2. _____
3. _____
4. _____
5. _____

28 Unit 3 | Change My World, Change Our World

Name: _____ Group: _____ Date: _____

6 _____
_____

7 _____
_____

8 _____
_____

9 _____
_____

10 _____
_____

Strategy

11 Using Gestures

When you don't know a word, you can often use your hands, your body, or your facial expression to express your words. The next time you are in a situation where you are looking for words, try using gestures to say what you mean!

› Read these phrases and mime these verbs to a partner to see if she/he guesses the verb you are miming correctly.

› Mime ten verbs each.

› When you are miming, your partner must close her/his Activity Book.

› Don't follow the same order suggested here.

- giving a flower
- picking a flower
- changing a baby's diaper
- combing your hair
- cleaning the floor
- brushing your teeth
- making a pizza
- driving a car
- opening a wine bottle
- drying the dishes
- preparing an omelette
- playing hockey
- making a fire
- chopping a tree
- riding a bicycle
- picking apples
- eating popcorn
- taking a shower
- calling 911
- swimming

Express Yourself Activity Book | Unit 3 | 29

Name: _____ Group: _____ Date: _____

12 A Cartoon Caption

This cartoon is related to the theme of the unit.

> Write a caption for the cartoon.
> Make your caption funny or original!

_____

Go Further

Have a class contest to vote on the best caption for the cartoon.

> Write your caption on a piece of paper (do not write your name), put it up on the wall and then walk around the class to read all of the captions.
> Decide which one you like the best.

My votes for best caption:

1st Place _____
2nd Place _____
3rd Place _____

30 Unit 3 | Change My World, Change Our World

Unit 4

Websites and E-mail: Use Your Judgment

 Structure

Articles

Whenever you want to talk about an object, an idea, a place or person, you will need to use articles in English.

Indefinite Articles (a, an)

Use **a**
 • In front of nouns that you can count (apples, dogs, …)
   I read **a** webpage.
 • In front of professions (dentist, teacher, …)
   He is **a** computer technician.
 • When giving the rate or pace of something
   fifty megabytes (MB) **a** second

Use **an**   • Following the same rules as for **a**   • In front of words that start with vowels (a, e, i, o, u) or silent "h" sounds   **an** e-mail, **an** evaluation, **an** old dog, **an** hour   **Exception:** If the "u" sounds like "you," then use **a**; if not, always use **an**.

Express Yourself Activity Book | Unit 4 | 31

Name: _____ Group: _____ Date: _____

1 A or An?

> Read the following sentences and decide if you should use **a** or **an**.
> Write the correct article for each sentence in the blank space.

Example: I received ___an___ e-card for my birthday.

❶ I created _____ quiz.

❷ I chose to make _____ poster.

❸ I made _____ information poster.

❹ I have never received _____ e-mail hoax.

❺ _____ hoax is a trick or _____ joke.

2 An Office Scene

> Write five sentences using the indefinite article to describe the scene below.
> Use the Smart Words to help you.
> You can use the simple present or present progressive tense.

Smart Words

nouns: woman, man, telephone, dead plant, watering can, open window

verbs: type, offer, ring, say, be

Example: A woman types on a computer.

❶ _____
❷ _____
❸ _____
❹ _____
❺ _____

32 | Unit 4 | Websites and E-mail: Use Your Judgment

Name: _____ Group: _____ Date: _____

s^ma^rt Structure

Articles

Definite Article (the)

Use **the**
 • When talking about something we have already talked about
     Do you remember **the** e-mail hoax I told you about?
 • When there is only one of it in the world
     the Internet, **the** sky, **the** Earth
 • In front of an important title
     the Prime Minister of Canada
 • In front of newspaper names, buildings, hotels
     the Gazette, **the** CN Tower, **the** Château Frontenac

3 Website Criteria

> Remind yourself again of the criteria that a good website should have.
> Decide whether to add the definite article or the indefinite article to each sentence.

Example: ____The____ facts are ____the____ same on many websites.

Who?

❶ _____ site has _____ good reputation.

❷ _____ person who created _____ site is qualified.

Why?

❸ _____ site does not want to sell _____ product or _____ idea.

When?

❹ _____ site was updated recently.

How much?

❺ _____ site gives _____ lot of information.

When Not to Use Articles

Don't use articles
 • For sports
     I play soccer, basketball and rugby.
 • For unspecific, plural nouns
     I love to eat strawberries.
     I ate **the** strawberries that I bought yesterday.
 • For nouns that we can't count (time, water, spam, information, etc.)
     We need money to buy snacks.
 • For most countries (unless their names contain a plural or they have an official title)
     Canada, Great Britain, Australia
     The United States, **The** Republic of China

Express Yourself Activity Book | Unit 4 | 33

Name: _____ Group: _____ Date: _____

4 Article or No Article?

Sometimes it is hard to know whether or not to use an article.

> Use the article charts to help you to decide whether or not to use **a**, **an**, **the** or no article at all.
> Write the correct word in the space or write **NA** (no article) if it doesn't need an article.

Example: __NA__ Canada has many __NA__ websites on __NA__ hockey.

1. It is not _____ good idea to forward _____ e-mail hoaxes because they may contain _____ false information and even help to spread _____ spam.

2. There are many _____ websites on _____ sports such as _____ soccer, _____ baseball and _____ cricket.

3. Many _____ activists spread _____ information about _____ Tibet through _____ Internet. For example, _____ Chinese Government claims that _____ Tibet is part of _____ Republic of China. _____ United States and _____ Europe do not agree with China. Through websites, they support _____ Tibet and its spiritual leader, _____ Dalai Lama.

4. When you edit _____ project, you should pay attention to _____ evaluation criteria. In this unit, you need to use _____ articles properly and make sure your _____ ideas make sense before you write _____ clean copy.

Smart Words

chain letter   tracker
hoax   forward
harm   database
spam   wish

5 Match It

> Read the following definitions.
> Write the Smart Word that matches each definition.

1. Large amount of information stored on a computer system: _____

2. Desire for something: _____

3. Damage or hurt: _____

4. Trick or deception: _____

5. Letter that asks you to forward it to someone else: _____

6. Something or someone that follows the path of something: _____

7. To pass something on; give it to someone else: _____

8. Unwanted e-mail messages: _____

Unit 4 | Websites and E-mail: Use Your Judgment

Name: _____ Group: _____ Date: _____

6 Word Search

> Find the Smart Words in this word search.

> When you are finished, use the extra letters to answer this mystery question:
"What should you always do when you are on the Internet?"

S	H	U	S	E	Y	H	O	H	Z	U	E
P	S	R	J	C	O	F	U	A	K	D	C
A	I	D	O	A	O	G	M	R	N	M	A
M	W	A	X	R	E	B	N	M	I	S	F
T	T	T	W	L	O	E	I	W	R	P	R
C	H	A	I	N	L	E	T	T	E	R	U
N	R	B	I	D	J	H	R	P	C	E	S
D	O	A	L	L	S	W	O	G	I	A	E
G	U	S	R	E	K	C	A	R	T	D	R
M	P	E	J	H	S	E	P	A	R	C	S
D	E	T	N	A	R	G	T	T	C	V	E
N	T	A	H	K	T	G	G	W	O	D	W

chain letter	coat	database	forward	granted
harm	hoax	ice rink	resurface	scrapes
spam	spread	tracker	wish	Zamboni

___ ___

Express Yourself Activity Book | Unit 4 | 35

Name: _____ Group: _____ Date: _____

7 Computer Viruses

People talk a lot about computer **viruses** but what are they, exactly?

> Read the text below to learn more.
> Use your Smart Words to help you.

Smart Words

worm = a type of computer virus that is spread through e-mail

dealt (to deal) = to take part in

pranks = trick or joke

steal = take something that is not yours

link = connection

---

1 A computer virus acts like a biological virus. A biological virus spreads from person to person or from animal to animal, by penetrating living cells. A computer virus is a virus that passes from computer to computer, "infecting" a computer system or database. The infected computer, just like an infected animal, is called a "host."

2 Rich Skrenta, a high-school student, wrote a program called "Elk Cloner" in 1982. It was spread by floppy disk. Rich originally created this virus as a hoax. He put it onto a game. When you played the game everything was normal, but after 50 times the game did not open. Instead, the computer showed a blank screen that read a poem about the virus named Elk Cloner. The computer was then infected.

3 Before the Internet became popular, most viruses spread on floppy disks. Today, a computer virus can be transmitted in many ways, including instant messaging, chain letters and spam. We do not have a perfect way to track where viruses come from, but computer programmers are working to find a way to grant us this wish.

4 People write viruses for many reasons: as projects, pranks, vandalism, to attack the products of specific companies, to distribute political messages, and to steal people's personal information. Some virus writers consider their creations to be works of art, and see virus-writing as a creative hobby. But viruses cause a lot of harm. Releasing computer viruses is a crime.

36 Unit 4 | Websites and E-mail: Use Your Judgment

Name: _____ Group: _____ Date: _____

_____
_____

5 If you are working or playing on your computer and it starts to act strangely, you may have a virus. The first thing to do is to open the virus scanner program on your computer and run it. If that doesn't work, then go to the virus scanner company's website to get a more recent version of the software or call them on the phone to get help. You might have to take your computer into a computer store where an expert can help you. The best way to prevent viruses is to have an up-to-date version of the virus scanning software and not to open files or links that people send you without knowing what they are first!

8 Paragraph Titles

When the text in Activity 7 was originally written, it had titles for each paragraph.

> Look at the titles below and match them to the paragraph in Activity 7 to which they belong.
> Write the correct paragraph title in the space above the paragraph.

Titles

1 When was the first computer virus created? _____

2 Why do people create computer viruses? _____

3 What can I do if I think I have a virus? _____

4 How do viruses spread? _____

5 What is a computer virus? _____

9 Smart Words and Articles

> Answer the following questions about Smart Words and articles in the text you read.

1 Look at the Smart Words from Activity 6 on page 35. Circle all the Smart Words from that activity that you found in this text. How many did you find? _____

2 Underline all the articles. How many did you find? _____

3 Which paragraph had the most articles? _____

4 Which paragraph had the most indefinite articles? _____

5 Is the information that this paragraph gives general or specific? _____

Express Yourself Activity Book | Unit 4 | 37

Name: _____ Group: _____ Date: _____

Strategy

10 Planning

One of the best ways to achieve your goal is to have a plan. What do you need to do to get from where you are now to where you want to be? Taking a few minutes to plan out your ideas can save you hours of time later! Try writing a simple plan by creating a "To Do" list.

> Look at this "To Do" list for writing a story.
> Number the "To Do" items in the order in which you would do them.

_____ Ask a friend to read over your story and give you suggestions.

_____ Make changes to your story.

_____ Think of ideas for the story.

_____ Write a rough draft.

_____ Put your ideas in order.

_____ Write a clean copy of your story.

_____ Check your Smart Structures.

Now, imagine that your computer has been infected with a virus! What should you do to solve the problem? How do you know that it is a virus? What do you try first? Who do you ask for help? Where do you take your computer? What do you do to make sure that your computer won't get infected again?

> Use what you learned in the text to help you make a "To Do" list with five steps here:

❶ _____
_____

❷ _____
_____

❸ _____
_____

❹ _____
_____

❺ _____
_____

Unit 4 | Websites and E-mail: Use Your Judgment

Name: _____ Group: _____ Date: _____

11 My Virus

Did you ever have a computer virus before? What happened? What part of your computer was attacked? Did you lose an important piece of work? Did some important software stop functioning? How did you react? Were you angry? Did you think it was funny? How did you solve the problem?

> Write a short story (true or false) about a time when you were "attacked" by a computer virus.
> Write at least ten sentences.
> Pay attention to how you use your articles.
> Try to use Smart Words from this unit.
> Read the beginning of the story and the end of the story.
> Plan some events for your story before writing.

It was Saturday morning. I was sitting in front of my computer. I was _____

_____

_____

_____

_____

_____

_____

_____

_____

_____

_____

_____

_____. So that is the reason why I could not do my English homework this weekend. Can I please hand it in tomorrow instead?

Express Yourself Activity Book | Unit 4 | 39

Name: _____ Group: _____ Date: _____

12 Malware and Viruses

This unit dealt a lot with hoaxes and spam. You probably already know that one of the big risks of forwarding e-mails is that you could be spreading viruses or other **malware**.

> Answer the following questions about the word **malware**.

❶ Think about the word **malware**. What do you think it means? Take a guess here:
_____

Now look carefully at the word again. Let's break it up into two parts:
    mal + ware

❷ What does the word **mal** mean in French? Give the equivalent word in English: _____

❸ These words include the root word **ware**. Look at their definitions:
    dinnerware = utensils and tools for eating (plates, knifes, forks …)
    software = programs used by a computer to do a task
    hardware = computer machinery and equipment or tools for your home and garden

Can you give a definition for the root word **ware**? _____

❹ Now, let's put them together: **mal** = _____ + **ware** = _____

❺ What do you think **malware** does on a computer? _____
_____

13 A Cartoon Caption

This cartoon is related to the theme of the unit.

> Write a caption for the cartoon.
> Make your caption funny or original!

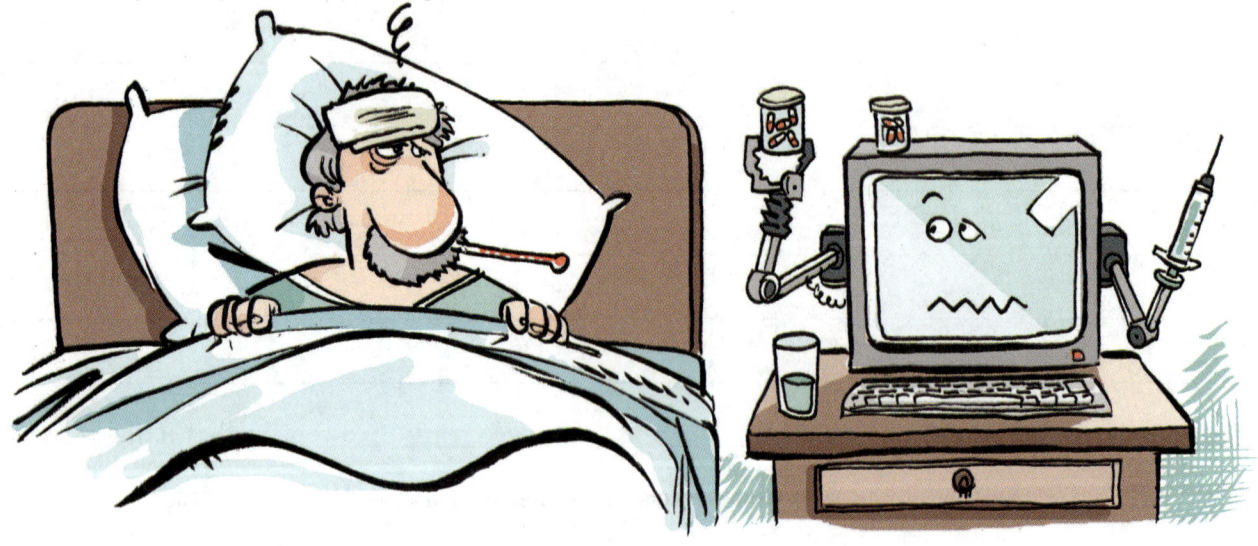

_____

40   Unit 4 | Websites and E-mail: Use Your Judgment

Unit 5

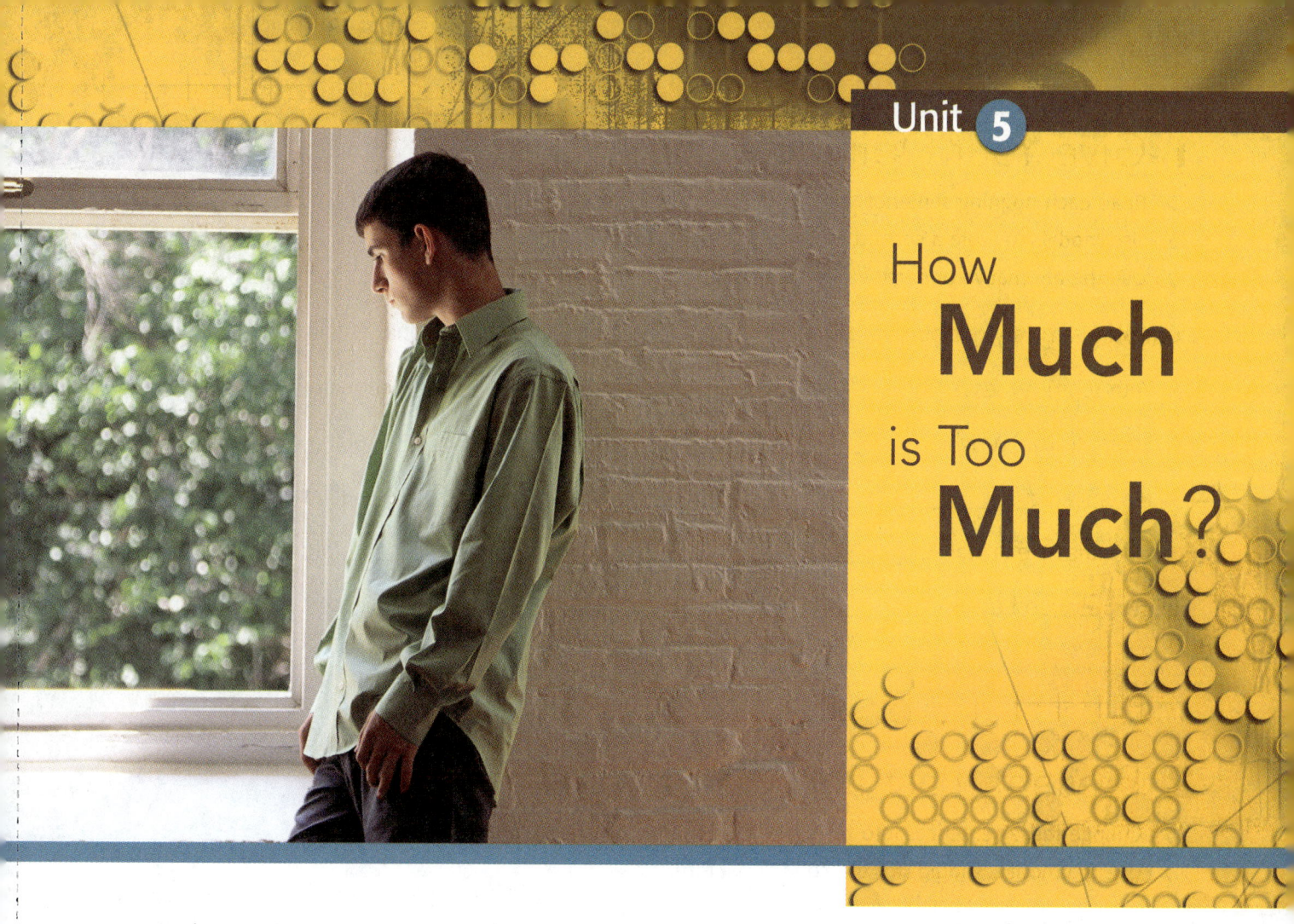

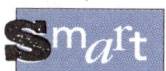

How Much is Too Much?

smart Structure

Modals and Conditional Form

Modals are auxiliary verbs that can be used with another verb to express a possibility, an opinion, or to give advice.

- Use **would** for general possibilities.
  Examples: I **would** like to see you tonight. I **would** speak Spanish if I practised often.

- Use **could** when you want to express a capability or be polite.
  Examples: You **could** run very fast when you were young. **Could** you pass me the salt, please?

- Use **should** when you want to give advice.
  Examples: She **should** stop smoking. My brother **should** study more.

Affirmative	Negative	Question
I **would** go to the gym every day.	I **would not** go to the gym every day. (wouldn't)	**Would** you go to the gym every day?
I **could** stop smoking.	I **could not** stop smoking. (couldn't)	**Could** you stop smoking?
I **should** stop smoking.	I **should not** smoke. (shouldn't)	**Shouldn't** you stop smoking?

Express Yourself Activity Book | Unit 5

Name: _____ Group: _____ Date: _____

1 Give Your Opinion

> Read each opening sentence.
> Use modals to write a second sentence that gives your opinion.
> Use the affirmative or negative forms, as shown.

Example: I am very nervous. <u>You should try to relax by breathing slowly.</u> (should – affirmative)

1. Your room is messy. _____ (should – affirmative)

2. I want to gain weight. _____ (could – affirmative)

3. He is tired. _____ (would like – affirmative)

4. Countries are at war. They _____ (should – negative)

5. This was too heavy. You _____ (could – negative)

2 Present, Past and Conditional Forms

> Change these sentences into the present, past and conditional forms.
> Use the modal "should" for the conditional form.

Example: Thomas (to be) influenced by his friends.
Present: Thomas is influenced by his friends.
Past: Thomas was influenced by his friends.
Conditional: (negative): Thomas should not be influenced by his friends.

1. She (to play) on the computer for three hours in a row.
Present: _____
Past: _____
Conditional: (negative): _____

2. Jenny (to train) at the pool every day.
Present: _____
Past: _____
Conditional: (negative): _____

3. My brother (to have) three cups of coffee before going to work.
Present: _____
Past: _____
Conditional: (negative): _____

Name: _____ Group: _____ Date: _____

4 My teacher (to shop) every weekend.

Present: _____

Past: _____

Conditional: (negative): _____

5 Your neighbour (to smoke) two packs of cigarettes a day.

Present: _____

Past: _____

Conditional: (negative): _____

smart Structure

Modals

Function	Modal	Examples
Possibility	**may, might**	I **may** go to the party.
Capability	**can, could**	I **can** stop smoking.
Permission	**may, can**	Mom, **can** I go out tonight?
Suggestion or advice	**should**	You **should not** drink so much.
Obligation	**must, have to**	You **have to** stop shopping so much.
Intention or promise	**will, would**	I **will** try to stop.
Politeness	**would, could**	**Would** you help me, please?

3 Use the Auxiliaries

Modal auxiliary verbs are used with the main verb to express many situations.

> Use modals to express the function that is required for the sentence.

Example: Permission: <u>May</u> I leave the classroom, please?

1 Politeness: _____ I help you?

2 Obligation: You _____ clean your room because it is a mess.

3 Intention: I _____ go shopping this afternoon.

4 Suggestion: He _____ spend so much time in front of the computer.

5 Possibility: It _____ rain this afternoon.

Express Yourself Activity Book | Unit 5 | 43

Name: _____ Group: _____ Date: _____

4 A Very Strict Mom

Joseph has a very strict mom. She has written a list of rules that he has to obey. Poor Joseph cannot believe it!

> Change these sentences into a question form.

Example: You must wake up at 6:00 in the morning to walk the dog.
   Must I wake up at 6:00 in the morning to walk the dog?

1. You must clean your room twice a week.
   _____

2. You have to study every night.
   _____

3. You cannot call your girlfriend.
   _____

4. You may not watch television.
   _____

5. You should eat only vegetables and tofu.
   _____

5 Lazy Stefania!

Stefania does not do anything around the house. Her parents allow her to do everything she wants but she is only fourteen years old. What do you think about that?

> Write these sentences in the negative form to find out what Stefania's parents tell her.
> Write both the long form and the contraction form.

Example: You have to go to school.
   You do not (don't) have to go to school today since you are tired.

1. You should do your homework.
   _____ if you don't feel like it.

2. You must help with the chores.
   _____ if you don't want to.

3. You have to vacuum.
   _____ because we know you don't like it.

4. You should babysit.
   _____ because we will give you pocket money.

5. You will ask us permission.
   _____ because you are old enough to decide.

44 Unit 5 | How Much is Too Much?

Name: _____ Group: _____ Date: _____

6 Word Guess

› With a partner, take turns describing the words in the list below. (Don't follow the word order given here because it will be too easy for your partner to guess the words.)

› Try to guess which word your partner is describing.

Example: "Ouch! My head! It really hurts!" (**headaches**)

binge	frozen	peer pressure
closet	headaches	shy
colds	interfere	spend
compulsive	laugh	thirst
drunk	lead	throw up
fashion	liver	wear

7 A Compulsive Shopper

You will read about a teenage girl who is a compulsive shopper.

› As you read, fill in the blanks with the appropriate word.

interfere	peer pressure
urge	compulsive
harmless	spend
closet	wear
fashion	laugh

Every Friday night, I hang around with all of my girlfriends. We have a lot of fun. We _____ all the time. We love _____ and we _____ cool clothes. My _____ is full. I think I _____ too much. I am a _____ shopper. I have the _____ to buy new things all the time. It is an impulse I can't control. It is not _____. I think the cause of this problem is related to _____. I want to look like my friends. My mother does not _____ because she is the same way.

Express Yourself Activity Book | Unit 5

Name: _____ Group: _____ Date: _____

8 An Interview with a Shopaholic

Shopaholic is another word to describe a compulsive shopper. Here are the questions we asked Joe, a shopaholic, to understand his bad shopping habits.

> Pretend you are Joe and invent the answers.
> Then practise saying the interview with a partner.
> Read both interviews: yours and your partner's.

1 Do you remember when this bad habit started?
_____

2 How many times a week do you shop?
_____

3 What do you buy the most?
_____

4 How much do you spend on average every week?
_____

5 Who pays for all of the things you buy?
_____

6 Do your parents have debts?
_____

7 How would you describe the shopping habits of other people in your family?
_____

8 What do you tell people when they ask about the things you've bought?
_____
_____

9 Do you ever lie about the things you buy?
_____
_____

10 What would you do to change your shopping habits?
_____
_____

Unit 5 | How Much is Too Much?

Name: _____   Group: _____   Date: _____

9 A Peer Pressure Story

This story will show you how important peer pressure can be.

> Read the following text.
> Underline verbs written in the simple past.
> Circle verbs written in the conditional tense.

Samuel could not believe his luck when his friend Alexandra invited him to Josiane's party. Alexandra was one of the most popular girls in school and she was also Josiane's cousin. Samuel had a major crush on Josiane but he was always too shy to speak to her. They were in the same English class but they never really talked. Josiane always sat in the front and Samuel always sat in the back with three of his friends. Maybe he would finally get the chance to talk to her at the party.

A few days later, Samuel was having a great time at the party, the music was good and there were many people he knew. Samuel talked to Josiane alone for a few minutes, which made him very happy. Maybe she would talk to him in English class now. He liked her so much ….

All of a sudden, Samuel saw that people were passing a marijuana cigarette.

"What are they smoking?" asked Sam, just to make sure he had recognized the smell.

"Just grass. Don't worry about it. My parents are not here," answered Josiane.

"Are you going to try some?" asked Sam.

"No, I won't. My parents are very strict," said Josiane. "But what about you? You should try it …."

Express Yourself Activity Book | Unit 5 | 47

Name: _____ Group: _____ Date: _____

10 Finish the Story

> Now think of an appropriate title for the story.
> Then add five more sentences to the story to end it.

Title: _____

Story ending: _____

_____

_____

_____

_____

_____

_____

_____

11 Understanding the Story

> Answer these questions about the first part of the text on page 47.

1. Who is Alexandra?
   _____

2. Who is Josiane?
   _____

3. Why did Samuel not talk to Josiane?
   _____

4. Where did Samuel sit in this English class?
   _____

5. Do you think Josiane smoked before?
   _____

6. What event made Samuel think that Josiane would talk to him in English class now?
   _____

7. What were people passing around?
   _____

8. What does Josiane say that Samuel should do?
   _____

Name: _____ Group: _____ Date: _____

Strategy

12 Practise

Did you know that practising speaking out loud is a very good trick to help you with pronunciation?

- Ask your teacher to read this script out loud to make sure you have the correct pronunciation.
- Then work with a partner and practise it many times. You can say the script in different ways: slow, fast, angry, dramatic.
- You can decide that your teacher reads the part of Alberto and the whole class reads the part of Gwendollina or you can decide to make teams of boys and girls.

Alberto: Gwendollina's friend
Gwendollina: a worried mom

Alberto: Hello?

Gwendollina: Hi, Alberto, this is Gwendollina!

Alberto: Oh, Gwendollina! I haven't seen you for such a long time. How are you?

Gwendollina: I'm not too bad. I was calling to ask for your advice.

Alberto: Yes, what is it? You can ask me anything, you know that …

Gwendollina: Well, I have problems with my teenager. She is always with her friends and I don't see her anymore …

Alberto: So what's the problem?

Gwendollina: I just told you. She is always with her friends and I am worried about what she does. When she visits her friends, I don't know what she is doing with them. Does she drink beer? Does she spend too much time on the computer?

Alberto: Gwendollina … Gwendollina … you worry too much. Your daughter is still very young …

Gwendollina: Yes, that's why I worry so much. When she goes out at night, I think about her all the time … I don't want her to do things she does not want to do.

Alberto: Your daughter is a great girl and you must trust her. You could ask her to call you when she goes out.

Gwendollina: That's a great idea, Alberto. I am happy that I talked to you. Thank you for listening …

Alberto: My pleasure. Call me anytime.

Express Yourself Activity Book | Unit 5

Name: _____ Group: _____ Date: _____

13 A Cartoon Caption

This cartoon is related to the theme of the unit.

> Write a caption for the cartoon.
> Make your caption funny or original!

_____

Go Further

Have a class contest to vote on the best caption for the cartoon.

> Write your caption on a piece of paper (do not write your name), put it up on the wall and then walk around the class to read all of the other captions.
> Decide which one you like the best.

My votes for best caption:

1st Place _____

2nd Place _____

3rd Place _____

© ERPI Reproduction prohibited

50 Unit 5 | How Much is Too Much?

Review 1

Name: _____ Group: _____ Date: _____

You learned a lot in the past few months! A good strategy to see how much you retained is to stop and check how much you can remember since the beginning of the year. These review exercises will tell you if you really understood some of the concepts, or if you need to take some time to revise and review. Take a few minutes to go through the work you have done for Units 1 through 5.

1 Simple Past: My Old Exchange Partner

Every year, my school participates in an exchange. Last year, we went on an exchange to Toronto, Ontario. Here is the profile of my old exchange partner.

› **Fill in the blanks with the correct form of the simple past tense.**

Past: Simon, from Toronto, Ontario

What I remember about Simon:

1. Simon _____ a cat. (to have)
2. He _____ to play card games. (to love)
3. Simon _____ a lot of movies. (to watch)
4. He _____ very funny! (to be)

My score on this activity: _____ / 4
Do I need more practice? (circle one)   Yes   No

2 Simple Present: My New Exchange Partner

This year, my school is on an exchange to London, England and I have a new exchange partner. Here is her profile.

› **Fill in the blanks with the correct form of the simple present tense.**

Present: Jen, from London, England

What I am learning about Jen:

1. Jen _____ to laugh. (to love)
2. Jen _____ the colour pink a lot. (to wear)
3. Jen _____ a lot of books. (to read)
4. It _____ a lot where Jen lives. (to rain)

My score on this activity: _____ / 4
Do I need more practice? (circle one)   Yes   No

Express Yourself Activity Book | Review 1

Name: _____   Group: _____   Date: _____

3 Question Formation

You are now thirty-four years old. Do you remember when you were a teenager?
How was your life when you were a teenager?

› Read this text.
› Read the questions that follow the text.
› Underline the questions that relate to the text.

When I was fourteen years old, I spent a lot of time with my friends. We spent hours chatting and sending e-mails, hanging out at the mall and having parties on weekends. Some girls in our class spent their free time gaming and making videos. They presented many projects in class. Our school organized several trips and we visited Toronto and Vancouver in the same year. We really practised our English that year. Our teacher showed us a few English movies. Starting that year, I noticed the soundtracks in movies.

Questions:

1. What was your teacher's name?
2. What did you do on weekends?
3. What did the girls in your class do in their free time?
4. Where did you hang out?
5. What did your teacher show you?
6. How old were you?
7. When did you go to Québec city?
8. Why did you sing every day?

My score on this activity: _____ / 5
Do I need more practice? (circle one)   Yes   No

4 Articles: Famous People and Famous Places

Last year, I moved to Hollywood and saw so many strange and interesting new people and places. Here are some of the things I learned.

> Choose which article to use: **a, an, the** or no article at all.
> Write the article in the blank, or write NA in the blank if no article is needed.

1. Ronald Reagan was one of _____ presidents of the United States.

2. He was also _____ actor.

3. He was also _____ governor of California!

4. _____ California is home to many famous people, such as _____ actors, athletes and politicians.

5. In 2007, David Beckham, _____ captain of the English soccer team, moved to _____ California.

6. He agreed to play _____ soccer for _____ "Los Angeles Galaxy" for more than 250 million dollars.

7. _____ Academy Awards (also called "_____ Oscars") take place every _____ February in Hollywood.

8. Only three actors have won _____ award for playing _____ role where they did not say _____ single word during the film.

9. _____ Capitol Records Tower, where many bands record music in _____ recording studios, is _____ landmark in Hollywood.

10. _____ tower can resist _____ earthquakes and it is _____ world's first circular office building.

| My score on this activity: _____ / 10 |
| Do I need more practice? (circle one)   Yes   No |

Name: _____ Group: _____ Date: _____

5 Yes/No Questions: After the Earthquake

Penny and Julie are two aid workers from Saskatchewan. They are in San Francisco to help people repair the damage after a major earthquake. First, they ask people if they are O.K.

> Look at the answer and use it to help you write a yes/no question.

❶ _____ No, I am not hurt.

❷ _____ Yes, they are lost.

❸ _____ Yes, I need help!

❹ _____ Yes, he wants water.

❺ _____ Yes, the doctors speak English.

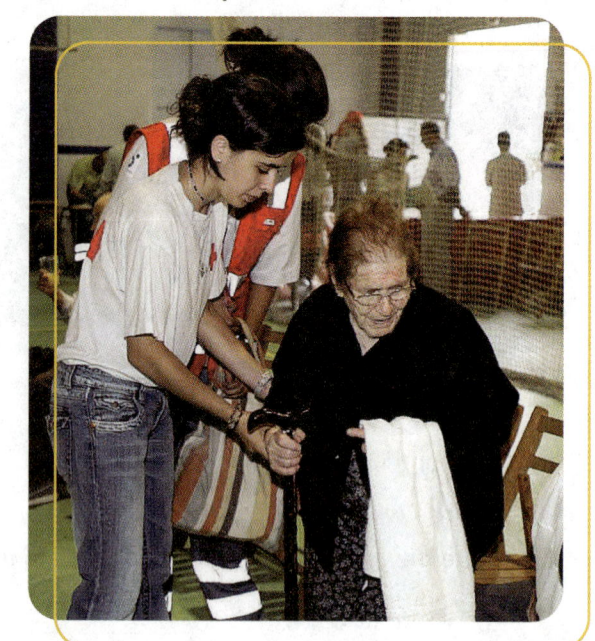

My score on this activity: _____ / 5
Do I need more practice? (circle one)   Yes   No

6 Question Words, Pronouns and Possessive Adjectives: What Happened?

Next, to help earthquake victims, Penny and Julie need to ask people what happened.

> Find the correct question word and write the appropriate pronoun or possessive adjective.

❶ _____ saved you? She saved _____ .

❷ _____ blanket is this? I think it belongs to Mrs. Peterson. Yes, it is _____ .

❸ _____ man is Tom's uncle? That man over there is _____ uncle.

❹ _____ did that lady give you? She gave _____ her jacket.

❺ _____ is your mother? _____ is sitting over there near the ambulance.

My score on this activity: _____ / 10
Do I need more practice? (circle one)   Yes   No

54   Review 1 | Activity Book

Name: _____ Group: _____ Date: _____

7 Possessive Adjectives: Whose Is It?

Finally, Penny and Julie need to help earthquake victims identify their possessions.

> Read the question and find the correct possessive adjective.

1 **Q:** Whose hat is this?
   A: It belongs to me. It's _____.

2 **Q:** Whose jacket is this?
   A: It belongs to my father. It's _____.

3 **Q:** Whose cat is this?
   A: It belongs to her. It's _____.

4 **Q:** Whose house is that?
   A: It belongs to Mr. and Mrs. Smith. It's _____.

5 **Q:** Whose book is this?
   A: It belongs to my family. It's _____.

My score on this activity: _____ / 5
Do I need more practice? (circle one)   Yes   No

8 Modal Auxiliaries: I Need Help

Your friend Moira is a computer wiz. She answers all the questions you have about computers.

> If the modal is used correctly, put a check in the **Correct** column.
> If the modal is used incorrectly, put a check in the **Incorrect** column and fix the modal in the **Changes** column.

	Correct	Incorrect	Changes
You: Do I **must** save my work every ten minutes?			
Moira: You **should** save your work often so that you don't lose it!			
You: If I **could** like to get some free games, where can I go?			
Moira: You **could** get some free games on the Internet.			
You: I am scared that my computer **must** get a virus!			
Moira: You **would** buy an anti-virus program to protect your computer.			
You: If I send this e-mail hoax, could I be doing something dangerous?			
Moira: Yes, you **could** be doing something dangerous.			

My score on this activity: _____ / 8
Do I need more practice? (circle one)   Yes   No

Express Yourself Activity Book | Review 1

Name: _____ Group: _____ Date: _____

Self-Evaluation

> First, calculate your score for the activities you completed.

1. My Old Exchange Partner: _____ / 4
2. My New Exchange Partner: _____ / 4
3. Question Formation: _____ / 5
4. Famous People and Famous Places: _____ / 10
5. After the Earthquake: _____ / 5
6. What Happened? _____ / 10
7. Whose Is It?: _____ / 5
8. I Need Help: _____ / 8

My total score: _____ / 51 = _____ %

> Then answer these questions to evaluate what you learned.
> Check all the responses that apply to you.

1. What Smart Structure are you good at?
   - ☐ Simple Present
   - ☐ Simple Past
   - ☐ Modals
   - ☐ Questions
   - ☐ Pronouns and Possessive Adjectives

2. What Smart Structure do you still need to review?
   - ☐ Simple Present
   - ☐ Simple Past
   - ☐ Modals
   - ☐ Questions
   - ☐ Pronouns and Possessive Adjectives

3. How will you review these Smart Structures now?
   - ☐ I will go back and look at the rules again in the Student Book.
   - ☐ I will ask my teacher or someone else for help explaining the rules to me.
   - ☐ I will do some more exercises to practise.

Review 1 | Activity Book

Unit 6

Are You Game to Learn?

smart Structure

Present Progressive Tense

Present Progressive

Use the present progressive:
• To describe an action taking place right now.
  He **is sleeping** now. Don't wake him up!
• To describe an action that will take place in the near future.
  I **am cooking** tonight.

Affirmative		
subject	verb "to be"	infinitive verb + ing
She	is	talking.

Negative (contraction)			
subject	verb "to be"	not	infinitive verb + ing
Dany	is	not (isn't)	listening.

Question			
verb "to be"	subject	infinitive verb + ing	rest of the sentence
Are	you	watching	a movie?

Express Yourself Activity Book | Unit 6 | 57

Name: _____ Group: _____ Date: _____

1 The Learning Lab

Welcome to the Learning Lab, where scientists are observing children playing video games to see if they are learning from the games.

› Read the scientists' notes and put the verbs into the present progressive tense.
› Then identify the actions that describe positive skills the children are learning by putting a checkmark next to the sentence.

Example: They (to cooperate) ____*are cooperating*____ together. ✓

	Observations:	Learning?
1	They (to play) _____ a game.	☐
2	He (to close) _____ his eyes.	☐
3	They (to look) _____ for clues.	☐
4	He (to relax) _____ .	☐
5	They (to take) _____ notes.	☐

2 Present vs. Present Progressive: Play to Win

Today in the Learning Lab, students are trying to figure out how to win at the new game, "The English Empire."

› Help them by choosing the right verb tense(s).
› Circle the letter of the correct answer.
› Note that, as in a real game, the level of difficulty gets harder as you progress.

Example: Jake: I _____ what to do first.

   a) am knowing
   (b) know
   c) do know
   d) knew

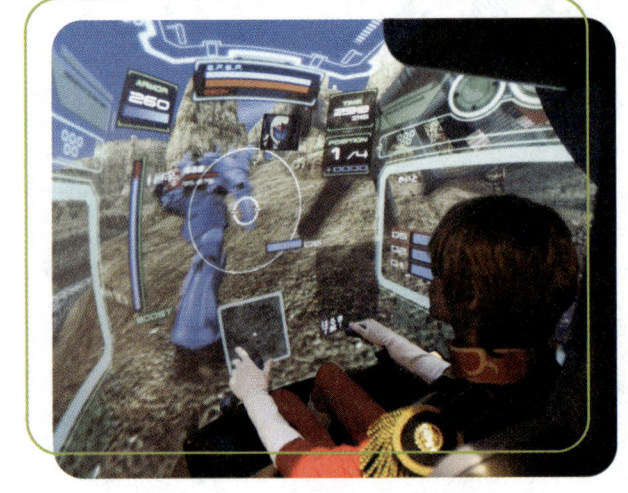

Level One

❶ Laurent: This game _____ interesting.

   a) is looking
   b) am looking
   c) look
   d) looks

58 Unit 6 — Are You Game to Learn?

Name: _____ Group: _____ Date: _____

2 Julian: I _____ .
I _____ it will be fun!

a) is agreeing / is thinking
b) am agreeing / am thinking
c) agree / think
d) agree / am thinking

Level Two

3 Kim: O.K. What _____ the first question? Julian, you _____ well—please tell us.

a) is being / is reading
b) is / read
c) are / read
d) are / is reading

4 Julian: The first question _____:
"What _____ right now?"

a) is / is you doing
b) is / you do
c) is / are you doing
d) are / are you doing

Level Three

5 Laurent: That _____ a strange question!
I _____ to think of the answer.
I think it _____ …

a) is / try / is
b) is / try / are
c) are / is trying / is
d) is / am trying / is

6 Kim: Laurent, you _____ of the answer—that _____ the answer!
You _____ so smart!

a) are thinking … is … are
b) is thinking … is … is
c) is thinking … is … are
d) think … is .. are

Level Four

Now the game gets even harder! Put your knowledge of verb forms into practice.

> Fill in the blanks with the correct form of the verb.

7 Julian: I _____ (to know) what to do here. This _____ (to be) just like another game I _____ (to know). While we _____ (to walk) through the forest, we _____ (to look) for clues that answer the questions.

8 Kim: I _____ (to write) down the clues right now! If I _____ (to take—negative) notes, I _____ (to remember—negative) the clues. That is why I _____ (to be) so good at these games!

Express Yourself Activity Book | Unit 6 59

Name: _____ Group: _____ Date: _____

3 The Video Game Commentators

Did you know that there are competitions for video gaming? This year, they are so popular that a television station wants to show one of these competitions on television. The commentators, Jerome and Sandra, will tell you what is happening.

> Read the commentary.
> Write the present or present progressive of the verb in parentheses, depending on the context.
> Try to look for key words to help you.

Jerome: Sandra, there _____ (to be) competitors from several different countries here today.

Sandra: Yes, Jerome! In fact, I _____ (to see) Kwan Leung from Korea over there.

Jerome: Where?

Sandra: She _____ (to talk) to Douglas McGovern from Scotland right now. Douglas _____ (to stand) by the "Exit" sign.

Jerome: Oh yes! _____ (to discuss / they / question) their strategy?

Sandra: I _____ (to think / negative) so. They _____ (to be) rivals!

Jerome: The competition _____ (to start) soon! The announcer _____ (to announce) the names of the competitors.

Sandra: Douglas and Kwan _____ (to walk) toward their consoles now.

Jerome: Look! Kwan _____ (to look) worried.

Sandra: No, I _____ (to think) she _____ (to concentrate).

Jerome: Kwan _____ (to pass) Douglas very quickly!

Sandra: Now Douglas _____ (to catch) up!

Jerome: Wow! This _____ (to be) exciting!

Sandra: Who _____ (to win)?

60 Unit 6 | Are You Game to Learn?

Name: _____ Group: _____ Date: _____

4 What Did They Say?

> Read the text in Activity 3 again.
> Answer the following questions using the correct verb tense.
> Hint: Your answer must have the same verb tense as in your question.

Example: Who does Sandra see? *She sees Kwan Leung.*

1. Who is Kwan talking to? _____
   _____

2. What is the announcer announcing? _____
   _____

3. What are Douglas and Kwan walking toward? _____
   _____

4. How does Kwan look? _____
   _____

5. Who is looking at notes? _____
   _____

5 New Vocabulary Words

Test your vocabulary matching skills.

> Match the following vocabulary words to their definitions.
> The first answer has been done for you.

1. ache   _a_   a) pain
2. bored   ____   b) include
3. clue   ____   c) to get better
4. improve   ____   d) abilities
5. involve   ____   e) set a limit
6. nightmare   ____   f) bad dream
7. promote   ____   g) not interested
8. restrict   ____   h) confidence in yourself
9. self-esteem   ____   i) encourage
10. skills   ____   j) information that helps you to solve a puzzle or question

Express Yourself Activity Book | Unit 6

Name: _____ Group: _____ Date: _____

6 Are You Game to Learn?

> Find the Smart Words from the last activity in this word search.
> Fill in the blanks with the leftover letters to discover the secret message!

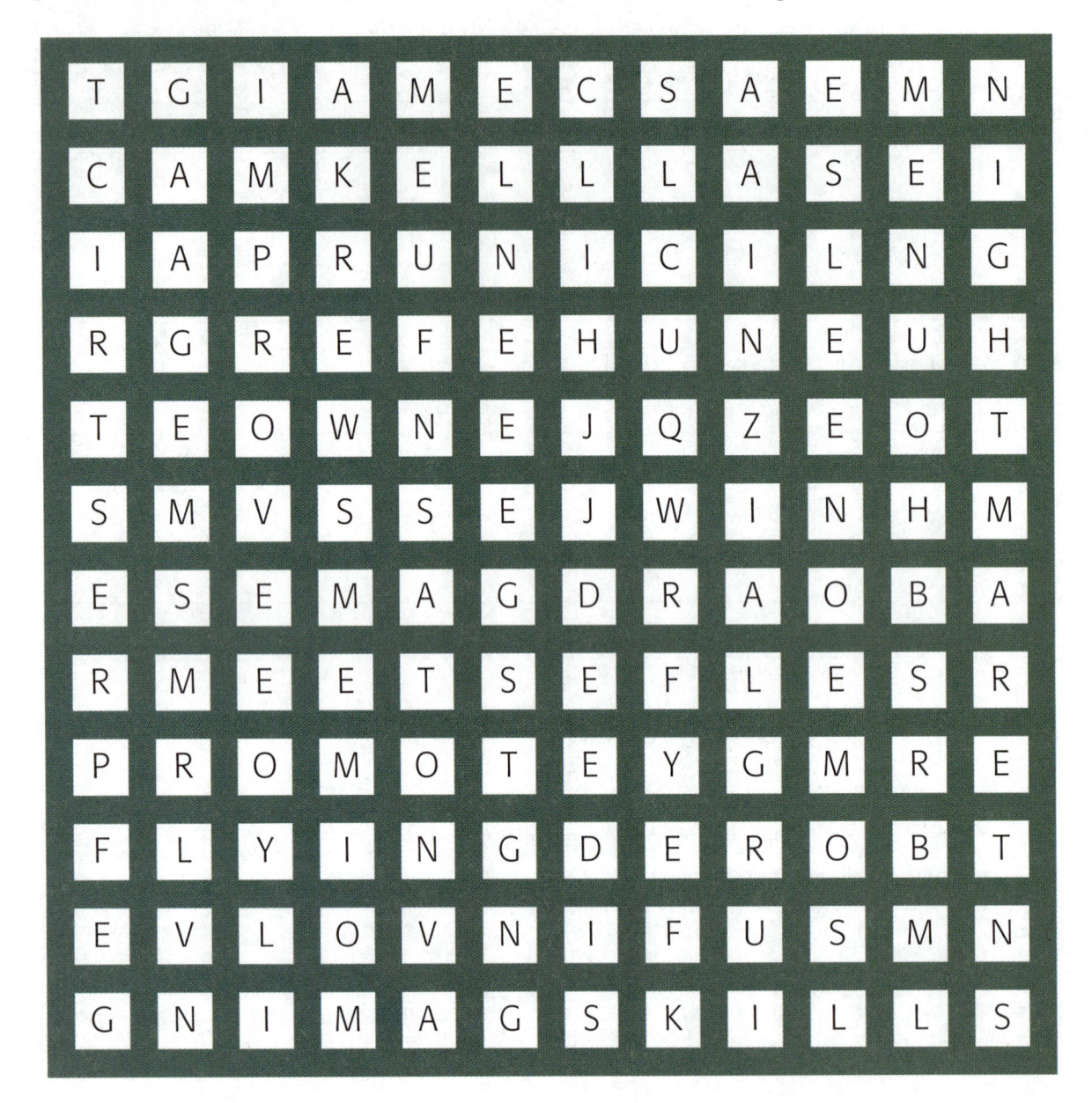

T	G	I	A	M	E	C	S	A	E	M	N
C	A	M	K	E	L	L	L	A	S	E	I
I	A	P	R	U	N	I	C	I	L	N	G
R	G	R	E	F	E	H	U	N	E	U	H
T	E	O	W	N	E	J	Q	Z	E	O	T
S	M	V	S	S	E	J	W	I	N	H	M
E	S	E	M	A	G	D	R	A	O	B	A
R	M	E	E	T	S	E	F	L	E	S	R
P	R	O	M	O	T	E	Y	G	M	R	E
F	L	Y	I	N	G	D	E	R	O	B	T
E	V	L	O	V	N	I	F	U	S	M	N
G	N	I	M	A	G	S	K	I	L	L	S

aches	aliens	board games	bored	clue
flying	gaming	improve	involve	nightmare
promote	restrict	self-esteem	skills	someone else

_ _ _ _ _ _   _ _ _ _ _ _ _ _ _ _ _   _ _ _!

Unit 6 | Are You Game to Learn?

Name: _____ Group: _____ Date: _____

7 Don't Blame the Game!

People today like to discuss whether or not video games are good for you, but then most people do not trust something new. Read about what people thought about dancing, novels, comic books and rock and roll music when they first appeared. You might be surprised at what you read!

> Put a check mark beside the strategies you will use before you read:

- [ ] Pay close attention while I read.
- [ ] Guess what the text is about by looking at the title and the pictures.
- [ ] Skim: Read the text quickly to get a general idea.
- [ ] Use resources like my dictionary and Smart Words.
- [ ] Ask for help when I don't understand.

Smart Words

novels = books that have stories about people who are not real
immorality = acts that are not nice or are wrong
entertainment = different ways people amuse themselves
waltz = a kind of dance invented in Vienna
ankles = the part of the body where the foot joins the leg
worship = to love and admire someone very much
labels = the paper attached to something that gives information about the object
R-rated movie = a movie restricted to adults.
careful = to avoid danger

Don't Blame the Game!

"They are immoral. They encourage our youth to spend all day inside. They teach young people bad lessons."

Did you think that these sentences were referring to video games? This is what critics said about **novels** in the 1700s! Today, it seems stupid to criticise novels, but 300 years ago, people worried that novels would teach children violence and **immorality**. In the year 2300, do you think that people will laugh at us for thinking that video games make people become criminals?

This is not the first time that people have criticized a new type of **entertainment**. In 1816, people thought that dancing the **waltz** would encourage sexuality—because you could see ladies' **ankles**! In the 1950s, people thought that rock and roll music made you want to **worship** the devil. For a long time, people thought that comic books encouraged teens to take drugs and become criminals. Of course, all of these ideas are wrong.

Today, a lot of people worry that playing video games will make children violent. What they don't know is that two-thirds of all people who play video games are over 18 years old. The average age for a "gamer" is 30! Video games can make people feel excited or aggressive, but then again, so does playing sports!

The solution to the problem is control: parents need to read the **labels** on video games and not let their children play games that are too violent. A parent would never let his child go to an **R-rated movie**, so they should be more **careful** about the kinds of games their children play.

Express Yourself Activity Book | Unit 6 | 63

Name: _____ Group: _____ Date: _____

8 Don't Blame the Game: Questions

> Answer the following questions about the text you just read.

1 What types of entertainment were people worried about?
_____

2 What is the average age of a gamer?
_____

3 Other than video games, what else makes people feel excited or feel aggression?
_____

4 Who and what is the solution to the "problem" of video games?
_____

5 Do you think that in the year 2300, people will laugh at us for worrying about video games? Why or why not?
_____
_____

9 WARNING!

Imagine that you are working at a store that sells video games.

> Write a label of one or two sentences for each of the following ratings.
> Make sure you explain why parents should or should not buy this game.
> Don't copy sentences off of the back of a game box or elsewhere—make up your own ratings!

Example: EARLY CHILDHOOD *You should buy this game if you have small children. It does not have any violence and is a fun game for learning. Children age one to five will like this game.*

EVERYONE _____
_____

TEEN (age thirteen and older) _____
_____

MATURE _____
_____

Unit 6 | Are You Game to Learn?

Name: _____ Group: _____ Date: _____

Strategy

10 Create Practice Opportunities: Use Your English Skills

You learned a lot of English in the past few months. Think about where you can practise your English skills outside the classroom.

> Answer these questions about practising English skills:

1 Name of a person I know who speaks English: _____

2 When and where will I speak with them in English? (pick one or more)
- ☐ at home
- ☐ at sports practice
- ☐ on the phone
- ☐ when he or she visits me
- ☐ when I visit him or her
- ☐ at summer camp
- ☐ other? _____

3 Where will I practise reading English every day? (pick one or more)
- ☐ in the street (advertising)
- ☐ in newspapers
- ☐ on the Internet
- ☐ in magazines
- ☐ other? _____

4 Where will I practise listening to English every week? (pick one or more)
- ☐ on television
- ☐ on the radio
- ☐ on the Internet
- ☐ at the movies
- ☐ other? _____

5 Where will I practise writing in English every week? (pick one or more)
- ☐ on the Internet (e-mail, blog, etc.)
- ☐ as a text message
- ☐ in a letter
- ☐ other? _____

Express Yourself Activity Book | Unit 6

Name: _____ Group: _____ Date: _____

11 Present Progressive Contractions

In English, we often use a contracted form of the verb "to be" when we are writing the present progressive tense. Simply replace the vowel in the verb "to be" with an apostrophe.

- **I am** playing / **I'm** playing
- **You are** writing / **You're** writing
- **He is** watching / **He's** watching

› Circle the correct form of the contraction in these sentences.

1. (Their / They're / There) walking to school.
2. (We're / Were / Weir) typing a message.
3. (Hes / His / He's) talking to his friend.
4. (She's / Sheis / Shes) doing her homework.
5. (Your / You're / Youre) listening to music.
6. (Im / Ime / I'm) finishing this activity.

12 A Cartoon Caption

This cartoon is related to the theme of the unit.

› Write a caption for the cartoon.
› Make your caption funny or original!

_____

66 Unit 6 | Are You Game to Learn?

Unit 7

Extreme Sports and Advertising

Smart Structure

Comparatives

In this unit we saw how some sports can be faster, more dangerous and more extreme than other sports. When we compare two things, we need to use comparative adjectives.

Comparatives		
One-syllable adjectives (big, fast)	**Two-syllable adjectives that end with "y"** (crazy, lazy)	**Three-syllable adjectives or more** (dangerous, spectacular)
• Add **er** at the end of the adjective, then add **than**. *This jump is **bigger than** that one!* *Luke runs **faster than** Gabriel.*	• Add **er** at the end of the adjective, then add **than**, and change the **y** into an **i**. *Charles-Alexandre was **crazier than** his friend Guillaume.*	• Put **more** in front of the adjective, then add **than**. *Skydiving is **more dangerous than** swimming.* *That jump was **more spectacular than** the last one.*
	Two-syllable adjectives that don't end with "y" (extreme, awsome)	
	• Put **more** in front of the adjective, then add **than**. *This half-pipe is **more extreme than** the other one.*	

Express Yourself Activity Book | Unit 7

Name: _____ Group: _____ Date: _____

1 I Am Better Than You!

Kevin and Cynthia are at a snowboarding competition. Cynthia is telling Kevin about her race, but Kevin only responds by bragging!

> Read the sentences carefully.
> Use them to help you fill in the missing words.

Example: I went **fast** in my race.   I went faster than you.

Cynthia: Hi Kevin! Did you just see my race? It was amazing!

Kevin: Hi Cynthia. Yes, I saw your race—it was **amazing**, but my race was _____ yours!

Cynthia: In my race there was a really **big** jump!

Kevin: Yes, but my jumps were _____ yours.

Cynthia: I went really **high** on my jump.

Kevin: I went _____ you.

Cynthia: Kevin, this was a really **important** race for me.

Kevin: My race was _____ yours.

Cynthia: Kevin, you shouldn't brag. It makes you sound **arrogant**.

Kevin: No one is _____ me!

Cynthia: EXACTLY!

smart Structure

Superlatives

Comparing two things is easy, but how do we say that something has more of a certain quality than anything else? We have to use superlative adjectives.

Superlatives		
One-syllable adjectives (big, high)	**Two-syllable adjectives that end with "y"** (crazy, lazy)	**Three-syllable adjectives or more** (dangerous, spectacular)
• Put **the** in front of the adjective, then add **est** to the adjective. *That jump is **the biggest**.* *That half-pipe is **the highest**.*	• Put **the** in front of the adjective, then add **est** to the adjective, and change the **y** into an **i**. *Tony Hawk is **the craziest** skateboarder.*	• Put **the most** in front of the adjective. *Skydiving is **the most dangerous** sport in the world.* *That jump was **the most spectacular**!*
	Two-syllable adjectives that don't end with "y" (extreme, awesome)	
	• Put **the most** in front of the adjective. *This skateboarder is **the most awesome**.*	

68 Unit 7 | Extreme Sports and Advertising

Name: _____ Group: _____ Date: _____

2 The Winners Are …

At the end of the extreme sports competition they announce the winners. There are three places: 1st place, 2nd place and 3rd place.

› Complete the sentence that describes the winners. Use comparative and superlative adjectives.
› Then write the name of the person who won each prize in the right place.

Example: *Category* **Height**   *Sport* **Windsurfing**

Ginny is **tall**, but Sara is ___taller than___ Ginny.

Shona is ___the tallest___ windsurfer of all!

3rd place = __Ginny__   2nd place = __Sara__   1st place = __Shona__

① *Category* **Strength**   *Sport* **Mountain Biking**

Solen is **strong**, but Veronica is _____ Solen.

Cara is _____ mountain biker of all!

3rd place = _____   2nd place = _____   1st place = _____

② *Category* **Speed**   *Sport* **Skydiving**

Ian is **quick**, but Bruce is _____ Ian.

Lars is _____ skydiver of all!

3rd place = _____   2nd place = _____   1st place = _____

③ *Category* **Talent**   *Sport* **Wakeboarding**

Sylvain is **talented**, but Pierre is _____ Sylvain.

Louis is _____ wakeboarder of all!

3rd place = _____   2nd place = _____   1st place = _____

④ *Category* **Dexterity**   *Sport* **Water Skiing**

Chantal is **dexterous**, but Annie is _____ Chantal.

Amelie _____ water skier of all!

3rd place = _____   2nd place = _____   1st place = _____

⑤ *Category* **Perseverance**   *Sport* **In-line Skating**

Fred is **patient**, but Philippe is _____ Fred.

Gilbert is _____ in-line skater of all!

3rd place = _____   2nd place = _____   1st place = _____

Express Yourself Activity Book | Unit 7

Name: _____ Group: _____ Date: _____

Common Exceptions	Comparative	Superlative
good I am **good** at skateboarding.	**better than** I am **better than** Hugo.	**the best** Max is **the best** skateboarder in Quebec.
bad It is **bad** to forget gloves in a mountain-biking competition.	**worse than** It is **worse** to forget your helmet **than** to forget your gloves!	**the worst** **The worst** thing to forget is your bike!

3 The Sportscasters

Stephanie Matthews and Dany Ouellet, are sportscasters covering this year's extreme games for Channel 12. During transmission of the events, the satellite cut out! Help us put back together the transcript of their sportscast.

› Fill in the sentences with the comparative and superlative forms of the adjective "good" and the adjective "bad."
› Decide which adjective is the correct one to use: good or bad.

Example:

Stephanie: Today is a ___good / bad___ day for snowboarding, Dany.

Dany: The conditions are certainly ___better than / worse than___ last year!

Stephanie: Yes, the weather is great! You could say it is ___the best / the worst___ day for snowboarding that we've had in a long time!

Which adjective makes more sense?
☑ Good   ☐ Bad

❶ Freestyle Snowboarding

Dany: This is the freestyle competition. The next athlete, Nancy Desjardins, is very _____.

Stephanie: Is it true that she is _____ last year's champion, Sonia Leblond?

Dany: I think so! I think that she is _____ freestyle snowboarder in Quebec! She will certainly win this year's competition.

Which adjective makes more sense?
☑ Good   ☐ Bad

❷ Monoski Event

Stephanie: This is a tough event, Dany. The monoskiers must be prepared for some _____ weather.

Dany: Really? What are they predicting? It can't be _____ having no snow, like last year!

Stephanie: No snow is _____ thing that could happen to a monoski competition!

Which adjective makes more sense?
☐ Good   ☑ Bad

70 | Unit 7 | Extreme Sports and Advertising

Name: _____ Group: _____ Date: _____

More Exceptions
If we want to say that something is not as good / fast / extreme, etc., as something else, we have to use special auxiliaries with our adjectives: **less ... than** (comparative) and **the least** (superlative). Hockey is **less** entertaining **than** snowboarding. Playing sports without proper equipment is **the least** intelligent idea I have heard of.

4 Training with Sandra

Sandra is a sports trainer who helps athletes prepare for competitions. Here is some advice she likes to give to her clients who are preparing for the summer extreme games.

> Unscramble the words to make a sentence.

Example: exercise / for / knees / your / the / biking / least / stationary / damaging / is

Stationary biking is the least damaging exercise for your knees.

❶ practise / tai chi / least / to / sports / dangerous / is / one / the / of

_____

❷ regularly / less / train / to / to / it / it / is / is / important / hard / than

_____

❸ prevent / less / to / than / to / one / treat / it / difficult / is / an / injury

_____

❹ eat / you / nutritious / the / bars / candy / are / least / you / food / can

_____

5 Vocabulary: Unmix and Match

In this unit we learned a lot of expressions that advertisers use when they talk about extreme sports.

> Unscramble these expressions.
> Then choose the correct definition for each expression.

To go as far as you can	Doing dangerous things
Go away! Useless	~~Don't get upset!~~

Example: have / don't / a / man / cow!

Expression: *Don't have a cow, man!*   Definition: *Don't get upset!*

❶ edge / on / living / the

Expression: _____
Definition: _____

❷ max / to / it / the / pushing

Expression: _____
Definition: _____

❸ space / much / up / taking / too

Expression: _____
Definition: _____

❹ leap / take / flying / a

Expression: _____
Definition: _____

Express Yourself Activity Book | Unit 7

Name: _____ Group: _____ Date: _____

6 Extreme Sports Crossword

> Fill in the puzzle with words from this unit.
> Use the clues to help you.
> Use the Word Bank if you are having difficulty!

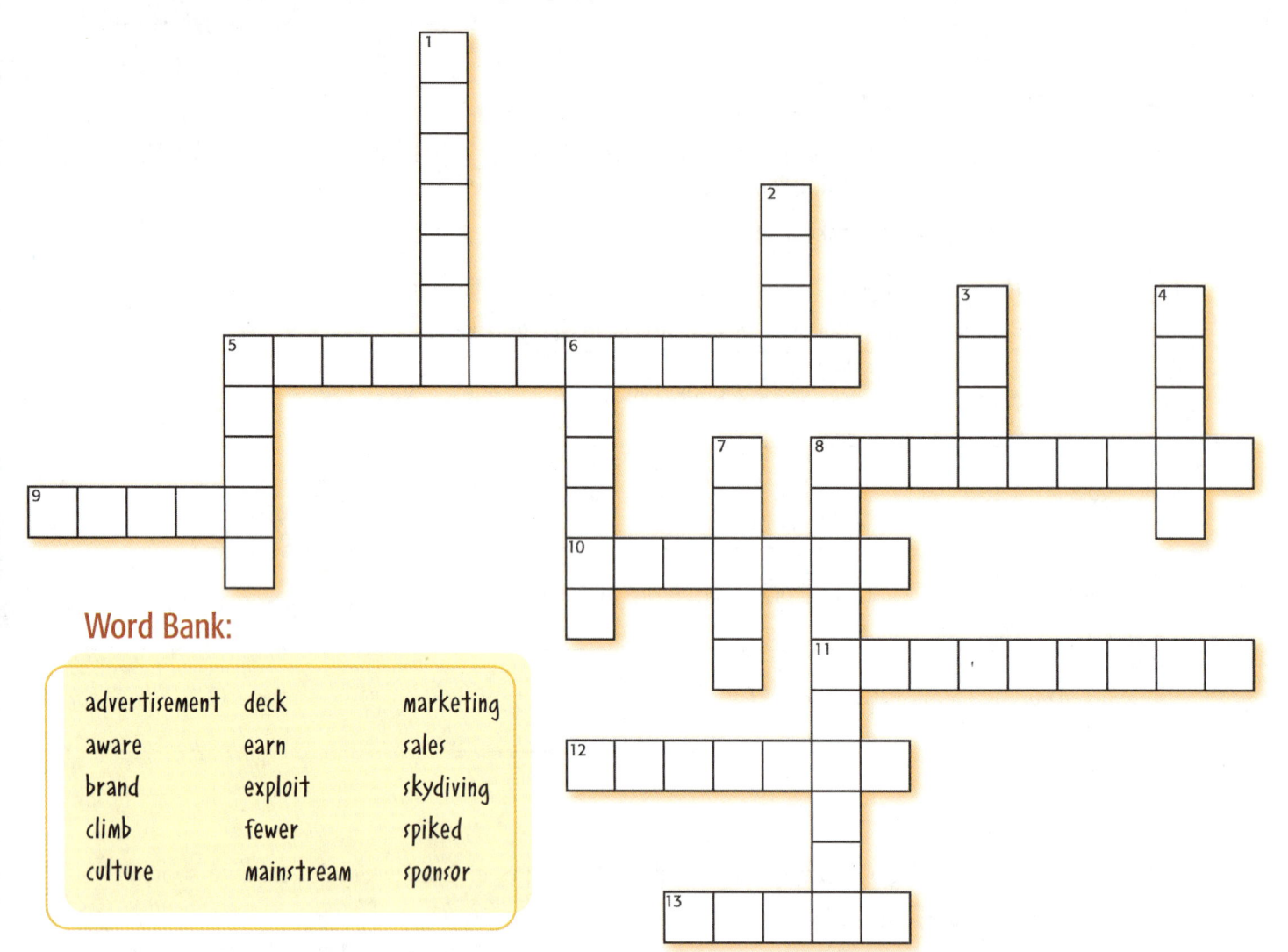

Word Bank:

advertisement	deck	marketing
aware	earn	sales
brand	exploit	skydiving
climb	fewer	spiked
culture	mainstream	sponsor

Across

5. Posters, videos and other ways companies sell their products to you
8. The way companies decide to advertise a product
9. Not many, less than
10. To use someone unfairly
11. A sport where you jump out of a plane
12. Ideas and way of life of a particular group
13. To move upward (like up a mountain)

Down

1. A person or company who pays an athlete money to wear a logo
2. To be paid money for work
3. The part of a skateboard you stand on
4. The name of a product that a particular company makes
5. To know about something
6. Pointed (like a punk's hair)
7. The amount of a product that people buy
8. Something that is done by most people is …

Unit 7 | Extreme Sports and Advertising

Name: _____ Group: _____ Date: _____

7 What About Television Commercials?

In this unit you learned a lot about how to make a poster advertisement, but have you ever thought about what you should do if you want to make a television commercial? What do you think will be important in a television commercial?

> Make predictions about what will be important before you read about television commercials.

> Check off the elements you think will be important.

- [ ] Using music
- [ ] Making a story
- [ ] Keeping it short
- [ ] Using colour
- [ ] Using sound effects
- [ ] Using humour
- [ ] Keeping it simple
- [ ] Thinking about who to sell to
- [ ] Using people
- [ ] Using celebrities
- [ ] Thinking about when to show it
- [ ] Other? _____

> Now choose the three things you think will be the most important in television commercials.

> Explain why you chose these three things.

1. _____
2. _____
3. _____

8 Making Television Commercials

Here are some tips that show what is important in making a commercial for television audiences. As you read, see if any of your predictions were correct!

> Read these tips and answer the questions.

Seven Tips For Making TV Commercials

1. **Who is it for?** Who do you want to buy your product? Women? Men? Children? How old are they? It is important to select a **target audience**, that is, the people who will buy your product.

2. **What do they like?** Now you know who you are selling to, think about what they like. For example, in a car commercial that wanted young Japanese women to buy the car, the advertisers included things young Japanese women like: beauty, food, fashion, design, creativity (photography, music and writing).

3. **Use people in the commercial.** Use actors from your target audience in your commercial. For example, if the product you are selling is a computer and the target audience are men age 20–35, include a cool, good-looking guy age 20–30 using the computer in your commercial.

Express Yourself Activity Book | Unit 7 | 73

Name: _____ Group: _____ Date: _____

> **4 Tell a story with words and images.** The story should be about how great the product is and how using it will make you smarter, sexier, cooler, etc. Use images that tell the story even if the volume on the television is off. For example, if you are advertising perfume for men, you can show a man using the perfume and then being chased by beautiful women.
>
> **5 Keep it short.** Most commercials are 15 to 30 seconds long. This is the longest the average person will pay attention. If your commercial is too long people will stop watching or the television company will cut off your commercial—even if it is not finished!
>
> **6 Use short sentences.** You don't have a lot of time! Keep your sentences short and interesting so that the people watching your commercial will remember them!
>
> **7 Think about music and audio.** Many people leave the room during television commercial breaks. Your music and audio should be interesting and tell the person about your product even when they can't see the image.

Questions about Television Commercials:

1. Look at your predictions. Which ones did you guess correctly? Which ones did you miss?
   _____
   _____

2. How long is the average commercial?
   _____

3. What would happen if your commercial was too long?
   _____

4. Who should you include in your commercial?
   _____

5. What is a "target audience"? Which tip gave you this information?
   _____

6. What story should you tell with your product?
   _____

7. Give the three tips you think are the most useful and explain why.
   _____
   _____
   _____

Unit 7 | Extreme Sports and Advertising

Name: _____ Group: _____ Date: _____

9 Do They Follow the "Rules"?

Let's put these tips to the test!

> Tonight, go home and watch television.
> Choose three television commercials and observe to see if they follow the "rules" that you just read about. (Hint: Try recording the commercials—it makes it easier to watch them again if you miss something!)
> Fill out this observation chart:

Observation Chart:

Date you watched television: _____

Time you watched television: _____

Who you think the "target audience" of the program is (women, teens, children, etc.):
_____
_____

Product #1 = _____

Product #2 = _____

Product #3 = _____

> Put a check mark on the chart for each tip the commercial follows.

Tip	Product / Commercial # 1	Product / Commercial # 2	Product / Commercial # 3
Who? (Does this product have a clear target audience?)			
What do they like? (Does the commercial include things that the target audience likes?)			
People (Does the commercial use people from the target audience?)			
Story? (Does the commercial tell a story?)			
Short? (Is the commercial 30 seconds or less?)			
Short sentences? (Does the commercial use short sentences?)			
Music / audio? (Do the music and audio keep your attention even if you leave the room?)			
Score: (How many tips did the commercial follow?)	___ / 7	___ / 7	___ / 7

Express Yourself Activity Book | Unit 7

Name: _____ Group: _____ Date: _____

Strategy

10 Encourage Yourself

Sometimes you may get discouraged when you are learning. It is not always easy to remember where you started from. The important thing is not to give up and to keep reminding yourself of how far you have come.

Here are some things you can say to encourage yourself and others.

› **Put a check mark beside the expressions you use as you continue to learn.**

☐ Don't give up! ☐ You are doing really well! ☐ Keep going!
☐ I am getting better! ☐ I did it! ☐ I can do it!

It is important to reward yourself for doing well. Each time you use something new that you learned, give yourself a little reward. Here are some ideas.

› **Put a check mark beside the rewards you will use.**

☐ Watch my favourite television show after I study for an hour.
☐ Congratulate myself when I use a new word.
☐ Tell someone I like about my success.
☐ My own idea to reward myself: _____

Congratulations! You are progressing!

11 A Cartoon Caption

This cartoon is related to the theme of the unit.

› Write a caption for the cartoon.
› Make your caption funny or original!

_____

76 Unit 7 | Extreme Sports and Advertising

Unit 8

I'm a Survivor

smart Structure

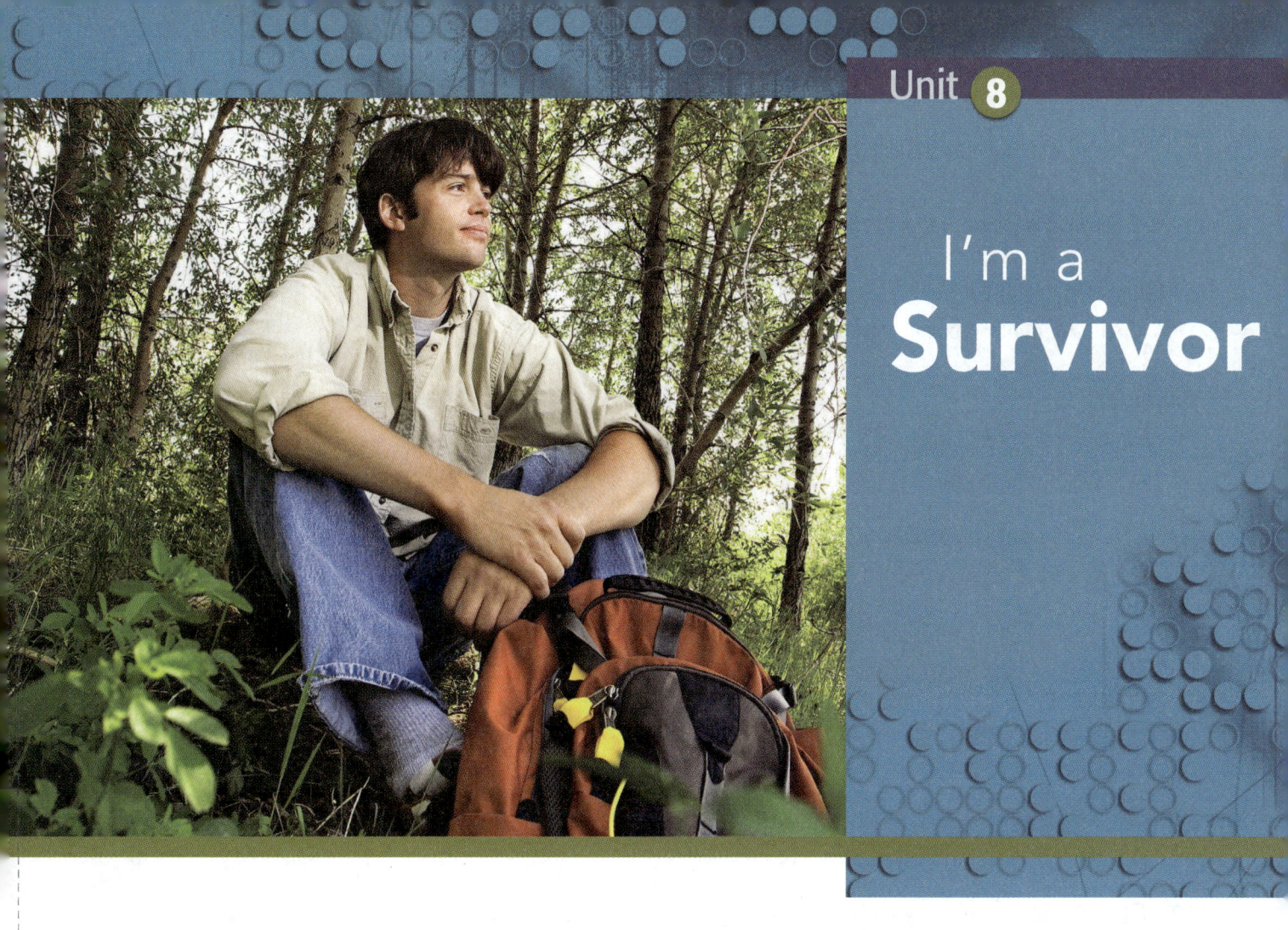

Prepositions

There are many prepositions you have to learn. Let's concentrate on three of them:
- **In** locates something in a large area / volume / time.
- **On** locates something on a surface or on a particular day of the week.
- **At** locates a specific point in space or time.

In	On	At
In the jungle	**On** the top of the mountain	**At** 1021 Seminaire Boulevard
In Peru	**On** this street	**At** the hospital
In the south	**On** an island	**At** the end of the road
In Montréal	**On** a boat	**At** twelve o'clock
In the car	**On** the plane	**At** home
In one hour	**On** Tuesday	**At** school
In November	**On** time	**At** the store

Name: _____ Group: _____ Date: _____

1 Lily and Joseph's Expedition

Lily Sinclair and Joseph Burns are two biologists who are going on an expedition. Before going on a trip, there is always a lot of preparation: getting the equipment ready, going to the pharmacy, getting a passport and so much more. Lily and Joseph hired a guide to help them. The guide calls them to get some last-minute details. Here are the answers to his questions.

> Circle the right preposition for each answer: **in**, **on** or **at**.

Example:
   Q: Where do you live?
   A: We live ((in)/ on / at) Chambly.

❶ **Q:** Where did you take your first-aid class?
   A: We took it (in / on / at) school.

❷ **Q:** Did you get your malaria pills?
   A: We will get them (in / on / at) the hospital.

❸ **Q:** When will you come for the last payment?
   A: We will see you (in / on / at) Tuesday.

❹ **Q:** When will you pick up your ticket?
   A: We will pick it up (in / on / at) a week.

❺ **Q:** Will you let me know if anything changes?
   A: Yes, you can count (in / on / at) us.

2 Questions for the Guide

Lily and Joseph wanted to make sure they got the best guide before starting their trip. Here are some questions they asked the guide.

> Fill in the blanks with the correct preposition: **in**, **on** or **at**.

Example:
   Q: Where did you learn your survival skills?
   A: __In__ the army.

❶ **Q:** Where do you usually work?
   A: _____ a national park.

❷ **Q:** Where did you start as a guide?
   A: _____ a mountaineering school.

❸ **Q:** When will we leave for the expedition?
   A: _____ a week.

❹ **Q:** Where is the camping equipment store?
   A: _____ the main boulevard.

78   Unit 8 | I'm a Survivor

Name: _____ Group: _____ Date: _____

s_mart Structure

Prepositions

Here are more prepositions to practise.

about	at	down	into	out of	under
above	before	during	like	outside	underneath
across	behind	except	near	over	until
after	below	for	of	past	up
against	beneath	from	off	since	upon
along	beside	in	on	through	with
among	between	in front of	on top of	to	within
around	by	inside	onto	toward	without
		instead of			

3 Find Pablo's Flashlights

Pablo is the guide of this next expedition, and he placed several flashlights inside the campsite. Can you find them?

› Look at the flashlights in the illustration.
› Use the right preposition to describe where each flashlight is.

Example: One flashlight is ____in front of____ the box.

1. One flashlight is _____ the backpack.
2. One flashlight is _____ the tent.
3. One flashlight is _____ the sleeping bag.
4. One flashlight is _____ the sleeping bags.
5. One flashlight is leaning _____ the tree trunk.

Express Yourself Activity Book | Unit 8 79

Name: _____ Group: _____ Date: _____

4 Practise Through Writing

The best way to practise using prepositions is to use them in sentences.

> Write a sentence using each preposition.

1. with _____
2. after _____
3. against _____
4. during _____
5. except _____
6. instead _____
7. since _____
8. toward _____
9. until _____
10. without _____

5 Which One Works?

These sentences were taken from the guide's logbook.

> Read the sentences.
> Then fill in the blanks with the correct prepositions.

Example: __At__ the top of the mountain, people cried.

1. We walked _____ the river _____ the mountain in one day.
2. The youngest participant talked to me _____ the problem.
3. The tree trunk room measured two metres _____ one metre.
4. Throughout the week, it rained day _____ day.
5. Salsa comes _____ Latin America.
6. The hiking group was motivated from beginning _____ end.
7. They preferred to pay _____ credit card rather than cash.
8. We started climbing _____ eight o'clock.
9. His wife stayed _____ home because she was too scared.
10. _____ the hike, people were singing.

80 | Unit 8 | I'm a Survivor

Name: _____ Group: _____ Date: _____

6 A Jungle Adventure

Lily and Joseph are in search of a special type of orchid that only grows in the depths of the jungles of Belize. They have just arrived in Belize and are meeting with a local guide who will take them through the jungle.

> First, read the following facts about jungle survival.
> Then read the text to see if Lily and Joseph are prepared for the experience.

Smart Words

clapping = making a noise with your hands
sting = pierce with a small pointed organ
vine = plant in the grape family
worry = to feel anxiety
yucca = food similar to a potato

Jungle Safety Tips:

- Never run from a jaguar. Walk toward it, shouting and **clapping**.
- Always run away from dangerous snakes.
- Stay away from most insects that bite and **sting**. Natives rub garlic on themselves to keep these insects away.
- The water **vine** grows everywhere in the jungle and is a good source of clean water.
- Palm leaves are good for building shelters. The Mayans use palm leaves to build roofs on their huts and these roofs can last up to fifteen years.

Lily: Joseph! It is time to get up! The guide will be here soon and we didn't even prepare our backpacks!

Joseph: Lily, you **worry** too much! I brought everything we need to survive the next week in the jungle.

Lily: I don't believe you, Joe. The last time we went on an expedition, all you brought was comic books and I had to share all my supplies with you.

Joseph: Yeah, well, I have learned a lot since then. Just look ...

[Knocking sound at the door]

Guide: Ms. Lily Sinclair? Mr. Joseph Burns? My name is Cesar Meaca. I am here to guide you to the jungle. Are you ready to go?

Lily: Please come in, Mr. Meaca. We are almost ready. Joseph was just finishing packing.

Guide: May I see what you are bringing with you?

Joseph: Sure! I am bringing only the essentials: my CD player, a flashlight, a tent, some chocolate bars, a rope and my notebook.

Guide: I think that the flashlight, rope and tent will be useful, but do you really need the other stuff, Mr. Burns?

Joseph: Please call me Joe. See, Lily! I told you I brought some useful things!

Express Yourself Activity Book | Unit 8 | 81

Name: _____ Group: _____ Date: _____

Lily: Yes, Joe, well done! But you still need batteries for your flashlight.

Joseph: Oh, I didn't think about that. Well, what did you bring?

Lily: I brought my sleeping bag, bug spray, lots of food and lots of water.

Guide: The sleeping bag and bug spray are good ideas, but in the jungle you won't need to bring lots of food and water. There are rivers and lakes to drink from and fish from. Also, we can eat potatoes and **yucca** that grow wild. Don't bring too much extra equipment—it will be heavy for nothing!

Joseph: I didn't know any of that! Thanks, Cesar. I guess we are ready to go.

Lily: I learned a lot of new things, too. I can't wait to go!

> Use the chart to fill in information about Lily and Joseph's expedition.

Good things Lily brings	Good things Joseph brings
Things Lily does not have to bring	**Things Joseph does not have to bring**
Things Lily forgot to bring	**Things Joseph forgot to bring**

7 Understanding the Text

> Answer these questions about the text you read.

1 After reading the safety tips, what else do Lily and Joseph need to bring?

_____

2 What new things did you learn about surviving in the jungle?

_____

3 Do you think that Lily and Joseph are well prepared? Why or why not?

_____

4 Would you like to go on an expedition to a jungle? Why or why not?

_____

5 Which tropical forest or jungle would you choose to visit? Why?

_____

Unit 8 | I'm a Survivor

Name: _____ Group: _____ Date: _____

8 A Jungle Postcard

> Write a five-sentence postcard from Lily and Joseph to their friends about their jungle adventure.

> To whom are they writing the postcard? Invent a complete address to write on the right side.

> Describe the best day of their adventure. Use the simple past.

> Use action verbs and describe their feelings.

9 Which Word Does Not Belong?

> Underline the word that does not belong.
> Explain why this word does not fit with the other words.

Example: skunk, bear, giraffe, rabbit, raccoon

The others are forest animals.

❶ river, sea, ocean, fire, stream

❷ hike, walk, swim, sleep, jump

❸ tent, hut, tarp, tepee, sleeping bag

❹ water, newspaper, oil, branches, matches

❺ desert, mountain, jungle, forest, Montréal

> Now correct your answers with the class.
> How many did you get right?

Name: _____ Group: _____ Date: _____

10 Picture Dictionary

Pictures sometimes help you to remember words better.

> Make a picture dictionary.
> Illustrate these words with your own drawings or with pictures from magazines or the Internet.

ankles	axe	clothespin	knife
matches	shelter	compass	cooler
mug	wrist	tent	toothbrush

11 Which Category?

> Put these words into the right categories.

- sleeping bag
- mirror
- tarp
- first-aid kit
- toilet paper
- water
- mattress
- tissues
- tent
- old newspapers
- map
- dry food
- matches
- bug spray
- compass
- small axe
- utensils
- can opener
- lighter
- air pump
- whistle
- knife
- flashlight
- plates
- sunscreen
- batteries
- canned food
- fishing rod
- mug
- towel

Sleeping	Making a Fire	Survival Equipment	Cooking and Food	Hygiene

84 Unit 8 | I'm a Survivor

Name: _____ Group: _____ Date: _____

12 Giving Directions

The survival trip is over, but you can use some of your navigation skills from the forest and jungle back home.

> Write the directions from the English classroom to other places in the school.
> Take your time. You can draw a quick map to make sure you are giving the right directions.
> Work with a partner. Your partner must visualize the directions you are giving and understand where your final destination is.
> Read your directions to your partner.
> Can your partner follow your indications easily? Will she/he get lost? If she/he can't, you need to make your instructions more clear.

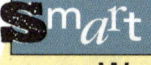

Smart Words
- go straight ahead
- continue
- turn left, turn right
- go up to
- turn
- go down the stairs
- go up the stairs

Example: How do you get from the English class to the school's exit?

When you leave the classroom, turn left and walk down the corridor.
Then, go down the stairs.
The exit door is there.

❶ How do you get from the English classroom to the school library?
_____
_____

❷ How do you get from the English classroom to the closest washroom?
_____
_____

❸ How do you get from the English classroom to the cafeteria?
_____
_____

❹ How do you get from the English classroom to the bus stop?
_____
_____

❺ How do you get from the English classroom to the principal's office?
_____
_____

Express Yourself Activity Book | Unit 8

Name: _____ Group: _____ Date: _____

Strategy

13 Practise

A good way to learn something is to practise it many times. Here are some tongue twisters that are fun to say and practise in camp.

> Choose one (or more!) to say as fast as you can.
> Have a class competition to see who says it the fastest without any mistakes!
> Ask your teacher to participate, too.

Peter Piper picked a peck of pickled peppers
A peck of pickled peppers Peter Piper picked
If Peter Piper picked a peck of pickled peppers
Where's the peck of pickled peppers Peter Piper picked?

How much wood would a woodchuck chuck
If a woodchuck could chuck wood
A woodchuck would chuck as much wood as a woodchuck could
If a woodchuck could chuck wood

Yellow butter, purple jelly, red jam, black bread
Spread it thick, say it quick!
Yellow butter, purple jelly, red jam, black bread
Spread it thicker, say it quicker!
Yellow butter, purple jelly, red jam, black bread
Don't eat with your mouth full!

She sells sea shells by the sea shore
The shells she sells are surely seashells
So if she sells seashells on the seashore
I'm sure she sells seashore shells

14 A Cartoon Caption

This cartoon is related to the theme of the unit.

> Write a caption for the cartoon.
> Make your caption funny or original!

Go Further

Have a class contest to vote on the best caption.

> Write your caption on a piece of paper (do not write your name). Put your caption up on the wall and then walk around the class to read all the other captions.
> Decide which one you like the best.

86 | Unit 8 | I'm a Survivor

Unit 9

Fear in the News

S**m**a**r**t Structure

Past Progressive Tense

Past Progressive

Use the past progressive:
• To describe an action taking place in the past during a specific time frame.
  *Yesterday, I **was writing** a test between 11:00 and 11:45.*
• To describe an action that was taking place in the past when it was interrupted by another action.
  *He **was walking** to school when the snowball hit hm.*

Affirmative		
subject	verb "to be"	infinitive verb + ing
She	was	talking.

Trick: It has the same structure as the present progressive.

Don't confuse the past progressive with the simple past.

The simple past is used to express an action completed in the past:
*I **watched** television last night.*

Key Words:
between … and …, during …, when … happened.

Name: _____ Group: _____ Date: _____

1 Past Progressive: Interruptions

We use the past progressive to talk about actions that were interrupted by another action in the past.

> Complete these sentences using the past progressive.
> Underline the second verb in the simple past tense.
> Then write the key word that tells you to use the past progressive in these sentences.

Example: You (cry)   **were crying**   when I saw you in the gym last night.

1. She (search) _____ for her keys when her mother opened the door.
2. I (take) _____ a bath when you called last night.
3. We (talk) _____ when the teacher came into the classroom.
4. The store (have) _____ a sale when she bought her computer.
5. I (shop) _____ with my girlfriends when he came to visit me.

The key word is: _____

2 Karim's Report

Karim Khan is a journalist. Yesterday, he was giving a report when something terrible happened.

> Read Karim's message below.
> Rewrite the message with the correct form of the verb tense (past or past progressive).
> When possible, use the key words to help you.

Example: Yesterday, I (to watch) TV when I (to hear) a sound.

Yesterday, I **was watching** TV when I **heard** a sound.

Yesterday, while I (**to report**) to you from the centre of the city, a bomb (**to explode**).

The explosion (**to happen**) at 11:13 in a café. The café (**to be**) filled with many people who (**to dance**) when the bomb (**to go**) off. Two people (**to be**) hurt and several others (**to be**) injured.

Just now, I (**to speak**) with an eye witness who said that just after the explosion, people (**to run**) around in the smoke. They (**to cry**) and they (**to shout**) for help.

Many people (**to hope**) that the violence in this city (**to be**) finally over, but unfortunately, this bomb has destroyed their hopes for peace.

Unit 9 | Fear in the News

Name: _____ Group: _____ Date: _____

> **Re-write the message here:**

_____
_____
_____
_____
_____
_____
_____
_____
_____
_____
_____
_____
_____
_____
_____
_____
_____

smart Structure

Past Progressive Tense

Making the negative form of the past progressive is easy! Just add "not" (or the contraction "n't") to the past-tense form of the verb "to be."

Negative (contraction)			
subject	**verb "to be"**	**not**	**infinitive verb + ing**
Dany	was	not (wasn't)	listening.

Journalists need to know how to ask questions correctly. We ask questions using the past progressive when we want to know what was happening during a specific period of time in the past.

Question			
verb "to be"	**subject**	**infinitive verb + ing**	**rest of the sentence**
Were	you	watching	a movie when I called?

Express Yourself Activity Book | Unit 9 | 89

Name: _____ Group: _____ Date: _____

3 Interview with a Firefighter

Geneviève Leblond is a journalist. She is in New York interviewing some firefighters about a major fire. Unfortunately, her facts are all wrong!

› Write Geneviève's question using the correct form.
› Write the firefighter's answer in the negative form.
› Then unscramble the firefighter's second sentence to find out what really happened.

Example: Geneviève Leblond: _Was the fire burning_ on all the floors? (The fire; to burn)
Firefighter: No, _it was not burning_ on all the floors.
(burning / the top floor / it / on / was) _It was burning on the top floor._

1. Geneviève Leblond: _____ out of the building? (the people, to run)

   Firefighter: No, _____ out of the building.

   (out of the / walking / were / building / calmly / they) _____

2. Geneviève Leblond: _____ ? (the alarm bells; to ring)

   Firefighter: No, _____ .

   (not / working / they / were) _____

3. Geneviève Leblond: _____ to the scene? (the fire trucks; to rush)

   Firefighter: No, _____ to the scene.

   (driving / carefully / were / they) _____

4. Geneviève Leblond: _____ ? (the people; to scream)

   Firefighter: No, _____ .

   (acting / they / normally / were) _____

5. Geneviève Leblond: _____ the fire? (the firemen; to watch)

   Firefighter: No, _____ the fire.

   (to / put / helping / it / they / out / were) _____ !

Unit 9 | Fear in the News

Name: _____ Group: _____ Date: _____

4 Who's Afraid of You?

> Read this news article.
> Fill in the blanks with the past progressive form of the verb.
> Answer the questions at the end of the paragraph.

Adults in England Are Scared of Teens!

Pedophobia. This sounds like a bad word, doesn't it? It is. It means "a fear of teenagers and children." The problem is that more and more adults have it.

Did you know that in 2005, more than 1,5 million people in England (to think) _____ about moving out of their neighborhood because "too many young people (to hang) _____ around"?

1,7 million people in England said that they (go; negative) _____ out after dark anymore because they felt scared of teens.

In fact, adults in England said that young people who (to stand) _____ around and who (to do) _____ nothing upset them more than neighbors who (to be) _____ too noisy!

79 percent of adults in England believe that young people were the ones who (to commit) _____ crimes, not adults!

These fears are not based in reality. Teenagers in England, like everywhere else in the world, are not more dangerous than adults. In fact, it is adults, not teens, who are responsible for more crimes around the world.

5 True or False?

> Use the text you just read to decide which statements are true and which are false.
> Write "T" for true or "F" for false in front of each statement.

1. ___ "Pedophobia" means to be scared of adults.

2. ___ Many adults in England wanted to move because they were scared of teenagers.

3. ___ More than 3 out of 4 adults in England believe that teens commit more crimes than adults.

4. ___ 1,7 million people are not afraid to go outside after dark in England.

5. ___ Teenagers are more dangerous than adults.

Express Yourself Activity Book | Unit 9 | 91

Name: _____ Group: _____ Date: _____

6 In the News: The Ice Storm

Do you remember the ice storm in 1998? Some regions did not have electricity for one complete month. Journalists covered this news every day on TV and in newspapers.

> Use the present progressive and the past progressive to explain each event.

Example: Present progressive: The ice ___is breaking___ (break) electrical cables.

Past progressive: The ice ___was breaking___ electrical cables.

❶ Present progressive: Schools _____ (close)

Past progressive: Schools _____

❷ Present progressive: Shelters _____ (give) blankets to people.

Past progressive: Shelters _____ blankets to people.

❸ Present progressive: People _____ (start) fires to keep warm.

Past progressive: People _____ fires to keep warm.

❹ Present progressive: The army _____ (clear) branches off roads.

Past progressive: The army _____ branches off roads.

Strategy

7 Take Notes

You are about to read a new text. One of the best ways to remember what you read or heard is to take notes. Here are some tips to help you take better notes:

❶ Each time you take notes, start on a new page and write the date—it helps you to organize later.

❷ Use a highlighter to highlight text or point to important notes.

❸ Write down the big ideas in a graphic organizer. Look or listen for facts and connections.

❹ Use abbreviations for long words. For example, government can become "gov."

❺ Leave space on the page to add information later on.

❻ Draw lines or arrows that connect ideas, sequences or events.

> Which tips will you use to take notes? Circle three that you will use.
> Write down at least five important ideas from the text as you read.

_____
_____
_____
_____
_____

92 Unit 9 | Fear in the News

Name: _____ Group: _____ Date: _____

8 Scary News: Bombing

Another Letter Bomb!

A letter bomb exploded in England on Tuesday. Two people at a business office were injured. This is the second letter bomb to go off in two days.

At 2:30 p.m., police and the ambulance got calls reporting a small explosion at a tax and accounting company in Berkshire, in the south of England.

Police said that two male employees in their 30s injured their hands in the explosion, but the injuries were not too serious. The men did not have to go to the hospital.

The British Army sent a bomb unit to the site while 14 people from the offices were waiting outside. No one was allowed to enter the area while police and investigators made sure it was safe.

"We were doing an investigation on the first bomb, when the second bomb went off," a police spokesman said, "but it is still too early to connect this bomb to the other bomb."

The first bomb exploded on Monday when an envelope in the mailroom of another company suddenly blew up. A female employee had minor injuries to her hand as a result of this bomb.

Police are looking for suspects in both bombing cases.

9 Reading Comprehension

> Use the notes you took to answer these questions.

1. Write two examples of the past progressive in this article.
   _____

2. Who is in charge of investigating the bombs?
   _____

3. Who was injured in the first bombing? Who was injured in the second bombing?
   _____
   _____

4. Were the injuries serious? How do you know?
   _____

5. How were the bombs delivered?
   _____

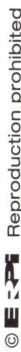

Express Yourself Activity Book | Unit 9

Name: _____ Group: _____ Date: _____

10 Find the Mystery Question

> Unscramble each of the Smart Words from the Word Bank below.
> Copy the letters in the numbered blanks to the Mystery Question blanks with the same numbers.

Word Bank:

alarming	broadcast	byline	caption	channel
collapses	commit	decrease	foolish	headline
homicide	lead	level	rate	reinforce
shut down	sum up	viewers	worst	youth

1. marmigla __ __ __ __ __ __ __ __
                           8

2. tascrordab __ __ __ __ __ __ __ __ __
                                  13

3. eylnib __ __ __ __ __ __
             17

4. topniac __ __ __ __ __ __ __
                    2

5. lanhcne __ __ __ __ __ __ __
                       3

6. seslolcap __ __ __ __ __ __ __ __
                                 9

7. omictm __ __ __ __ __ __
                       5

8. cadesree __ __ __ __ __ __ __ __
              1

9. lifosho __ __ __ __ __ __ __

10. naeledhi __ __ __ __ __ __ __ __
                      14

11. diicehmo __ __ __ __ __ __ __ __
                                 16

12. lade __ __ __ __

13. veell __ __ __ __ __
            7

14. raet __ __ __ __
          15

15. niereofrc __ __ __ __ __ __ __ __ __
                           18

94   Unit 9 | Fear in the News

Name: _____ Group: _____ Date: _____

16 suth nowd ___ ___ ___   ___ ___ ___
                    19   10

17 msu pu ___ ___ ___   ___ ___
            4

18 weevirs ___ ___ ___ ___ ___ ___
                               11

19 wosrt ___ ___ ___ ___
                12

20 tohuy ___ ___ ___ ___ ___
                      6

Mystery Question:

___ ___ ___ ___   ___ ___ ___   ___ ___ ___ ___
 1   2   3   4   5   6   7   8   9 10 11

___ ___ ___ ___ ___   ___ ___ ___ ?
12 13 14 15 16 17 18 19

11 Smart Words

> Choose eight of the following Smart Words and write a sentence for each one.
> Try to use the past progressive.

Example: I was scared when I saw that the bridge was collapsing under my car!

collapse	shut down	reinforce	decrease	sum up
blame	youth	homicide	backlash	deed

1 _____
2 _____
3 _____
4 _____
5 _____
6 _____
7 _____
8 _____

Name: _____ Group: _____ Date: _____

12 The Stanley Cup Riots

An editor was putting together a story about the Stanley Cup Riots for a newspaper when a virus hit his computer. The sentences for the story got all mixed up!

> Unscramble the sentences to complete the story.

Example:

the Stanley Cup / the Canadiens / last night / people / in / were / Montréal / celebrating / winning /

Last night in Montréal, people were celebrating the Canadiens winning the Stanley Cup.

1 streets / were / the / in / they / dancing

_____

2 were / people / violent / some / becoming

_____

3 windows / people / car / and / windshields / smashing / were / store

_____

4 pushing / crowds / the / were / people

_____

5 hard / to keep / were / the / working / police / control

_____

13 A Cartoon Caption

This cartoon is related to the theme of the unit.

> Write a caption for the cartoon.
> Make your caption funny or original!

Unit 10

Strange and Unusual Jobs

Smart Structure

Future Tense

There are two ways to express the future:

1 Use "will"
- To express a voluntary action
- To express a promise
- To express a prediction

Affirmative	Negative (contraction)	Question
will + verb	will + not + verb	Start your question with the auxiliary "will."
The security guard **will work** all night. My teacher **will call** my parents. The year 2222 **will be** a very interesting year.	I **will not work** tomorrow. (won't)	**Will** you **work** tomorrow?

Express Yourself Activity Book | Unit 10

Name: _____ Group: _____ Date: _____

2 Use the verb "to be" and "going to"
- To express a plan
- To express a prediction

Affirmative	Negative (contraction)	Question
verb "to be" + going to + verb	verb "to be" + not + going to + verb	Start your question with the verb "to be."
The cook **is going to cook** for us. I **am going to meet** my friend tonight. They **are going to be** there.	They **are not going to be** there. (aren't)	**Are** they **going to be** there?

Key Words:
today, tomorrow, later, next week, the next day, in a few minutes, then

1 Summer Plans

What are your plans for the summer?

> Answer these questions using the future tense.
> Write two complete sentences: one sentence using "will" and the other using the verb "to be" + "going to."

Example: (study math) I will study math so I can pass my summer class exam.
I am going to study math so I can pass my summer class exam.

1 (visit my grandmother)
_____
_____

2 (see my best friend a lot)
_____
_____

3 (go shopping)
_____
_____

4 (spend time with my cousins)
_____
_____

5 (read ten novels)
_____
_____

Unit 10 | Strange and Unusual Jobs

Name: _____ Group: _____ Date: _____

2 Emilie's Summer Job

Emilie wants to work a few hours this summer. She loves being outside. This is her plan.

> Unscramble these sentences.
> Then change them into the question form.

Example: summer / this / Emilie / have / will / a / job.

Sentence: This summer, Emilie will have a job.
Question: Will Emilie have a job this summer?

1. field / strawberry / a / has / who / aunt / her / call / will / she

   _____
   _____

2. July / June / to / she / is / work / to / going / from

   _____
   _____

3. She / every / will / day / work / 5 o'clock / to / 2 o'clock / from

   _____
   _____

4. weigh / strawberries / she / will / afternoon / all

   _____
   _____

5. strawberries / of / lot / of / course / she / going / is / eat / to / a

   _____
   _____

3 What Will Happen?

> Write the negative consequence for these situations, using the future tense of the verb in parentheses and the auxiliary "will."
> Then write the contraction form.

Example: If you don't do your research this week, __you will not finish (won't)__ (to finish) your report.

1. If you don't clean your room tonight, you _____ (to have) permission to go out.
2. If you don't study regularly, you _____ (to pass) your exams in June.
3. This year, if you don't speak English outside the classroom, you _____ (to become) bilingual.
4. If you don't eat healthy food, you _____ (to feel) very good in a few years.
5. If you don't train regularly, you _____ (to win) the marathon next summer.

Express Yourself Activity Book | Unit 10 | 99

Name: _____ Group: _____ Date: _____

4 A Dream Job

> Write five sentences about a dream job or something you want to do.
> Use the future tense.
> Make your text original!

My name is _____.

I am ____ years old.

My dream is to _____.

_____
_____
_____
_____

William Chocolatier
He will …

5 What Will Your Job Be?

What will you do for work if you choose one of these occupations?

> Write a sentence that describes what you would do if you took on each occupation.
> Write your sentence in the speech bubble.
> Use the future tense.
> Make your sentence original or make it funny if you wish!

Example sentence: A scuba diver: *I will study fish and coral.*

A plumber:

An artist:

An architect:

A dancer:

A clown:

A sailor:

Unit 10 | Strange and Unusual Jobs

6 Verb Tense Review

Here is a review of several of the verb tenses you learned:

Simple Present, Simple Past, Present Progressive, Future, Conditional.

> Read each sentence.
> Rewrite the sentence using the verb in parentheses in the appropriate tense.
> Then rewrite the sentence using the negative and question forms.

Example: Sophie (speak) five languages.
Affirmative: Sophie speaks five languages.
Negative: Sophie doesn't speak five languages.
Question: Does Sophie speak five languages?

1 You (call) me tomorrow.
Affirmative: _____
Negative: _____
Question: _____

2 He (be) here yesterday.
Affirmative: _____
Negative: _____
Question: _____

3 They (leave) school right now.
Affirmative: _____
Negative: _____
Question: _____

4 He (have) brown hair.
Affirmative: _____
Negative: _____
Question: _____

5 I (take) a bath if I had the time.
Affirmative: _____
Negative: _____
Question: _____

Express Yourself Activity Book | Unit 10 | 101

Name: _____   Group: _____   Date: _____

7 Children Who Work

If you work small jobs for pocket money, it may seem like hard work. But you are actually lucky if you are only doing it for a little extra money. Maybe you already work a little bit by babysitting or cutting the grass in the summer. Or perhaps you help your dad or mom with their business. But in some places around the world, millions of children have to work just to survive.

> Answer these questions before reading the text.

1. At what age do you think Canadian teens usually start working? _____

2. If you are younger than 16 and already working, what kind of jobs do you usually have?
   _____

3. Do you need to work in order to help your parents pay the bills? _____

4. Do any of your friends work? What kinds of jobs do they have? _____
   _____

> Read the text below. See page 103 for the definitions of the Smart Words.
> Try to visualize the story while you are reading.

Many children work. After school hours, children can help with household **chores**, run **errands**, or look after their younger brothers and sisters like you do every day. "Child **labour**," however, means something different—that children are doing things that are **harmful** to their healthy development. They work for long hours, sacrificing time and energy that they should spend at school or at home, enjoying being a child. In some very bad cases, they work in physically, emotionally and/or psychologically dangerous situations, putting their young bodies and minds under terrible stress that can lead to permanent damage.

How many child labourers are there? The ILO (International Labour Organization) estimated that in 2002, the number of children worldwide who were "economically active" amounted to 352 million. Of these, 211 million were aged 5–14.

Child workers are not only in poor countries. In industrialized countries like Canada, for example, around 2,5 million children aged 5–14, or around 2 percent of the total child population, are economically active.

Child labourers in Pakistan picking up paper waste from roads to recycle.

Unit 10 | Strange and Unusual Jobs

Name: _____ Group: _____ Date: _____

Smart Words

chores = jobs that are done in the house
errands = the action of going to get something
labour = work, especially hard physical work
harmful = can hurt you

8 Reading Comprehension

> Answer these questions about the text you just read:

1 Which sentence tells you what child labour is? Write it in the blanks below.
_____
_____

2 What is the ILO?
_____

3 How many children work around the world?
_____

4 Which sentence proves that this happens in rich countries too? Write it in the blanks below.
_____
_____
_____

5 What surprised you in this text? Write two sentences.
_____
_____
_____

6 What would you say to an employer who wants to hire a child? Write one sentence.
_____
_____

9 Smart Words

> Write a sentence using each Smart Word from the text.
> Use the future tense in your sentences.

1 _____
2 _____
3 _____
4 _____

Express Yourself Activity Book | Unit 10

Name: _____   Group: _____   Date: _____

10 Classifying Smart Words

Here are some Smart Words taken from all of the units in this book.

> Write each Smart Word in the proper column: adjective, verb or noun.
> Remember that sometimes, words can be both verbs and nouns.

Unit 1	Unit 2	Unit 3	Unit 4	Unit 5
skim	heart	neighbour	grant	spend
postcard	act	hug	spread	closet
sights	awesome	highway	harm	frozen

Unit 6	Unit 7	Unit 8	Unit 9	Unit 10
aliens	spiked	mug	alarming	scrub
skills	earn	shelter	foolish	owner
soldier	ads	teary	collapse	roller coaster

Adjective	Verb	Noun

104 Unit 10 | Strange and Unusual Jobs

Name: _____ Group: _____ Date: _____

11 Talk About It!

> Play this conversation game in teams of four, and give each player a game marker.

> Each player takes a turn rolling the dice. Move your marker the number of spaces that you rolled, and talk about the statement you land on. Give as many details as possible.

> If you land on "Free question," skip your turn and ask the other players a question of your choice. If you land on the bottom of an arrow, skip to the arrowhead, going up or down.

> The first person to reach "Finish" is the winner! If you finish before the other teams, start the game again.

Finish	Tricks to remember words in English	Why English is easy or hard for you	What you do each summer	Newspaper headlines
Your favourite music	Free question	Forest survival tips	Ads for products	An act of kindness
Your special talent	What you did last weekend	The nicest gift you ever received	Your weekend plans	Something you don't like to do
E-mail hoaxes	Video game strategies	Your ideal job	Smoking	Marriage
Free question	A TV program you like	How you get to school	Your room	What you do for fun
Your family	A country that interests you	Your favourite season	How to help others	A dream you remember
What you do after school	Your favourite movie	Free question	What you like to read	Your ideal pet
Start	Your best friend	A sport you like to play	Your fashion style	An English city to visit

Express Yourself Activity Book | Unit 10

Name: _____ Group: _____ Date: _____

Strategy

12 Substitution

Use substitution when you don't remember a word. You can use other words to describe it.

> Read the word definitions.
> Using the Word Bank, try to find the word that is described.

Word Bank:

| scrub | roller coaster | singer | make-up artist |
| storm | bleed | doctor | clown |

1. a person who transforms an actor's appearance
   _____

2. a person in a circus who makes you laugh
   _____

3. to wash very hard
   _____

4. strong winds and bad weather
   _____

5. a person who entertains with his/her voice
   _____

6. what happens when you cut yourself
   _____

7. a ride that has many loops
   _____

8. a person who cures you at the hospital
   _____

13 A Cartoon Caption

This cartoon is related to the theme of the unit.

> Write a caption for the cartoon.
> Make your caption funny or original!

_____

Unit 10 | Strange and Unusual Jobs

Review 2

Name: _____ Group: _____ Date: _____

It's already the end of the year! Let's go over everything you learned this year. These review exercises will tell you if you really understood some of the concepts, or if you need to take some time to revise and review.

> Take a few minutes to go through your Activity Book.
> Review the Smart Structure in each unit.

1 Question Formation: Nadine's Problem

Nadine's friends sent her an e-mail hoax that contained a virus! Now, poor Nadine cannot use her e-mail anymore.

> To find out what happened, write the answer that makes the most sense for each question word. The first one is done for you.

> Last evening
> The message had a virus
> At least five a day
> To her personal e-mail address
> ~~An e-mail hoax~~
> Usually at a quarter to seven
> Her friends send them
> Nadine's

1 What was the cause?
An e-mail hoax

2 Where was it sent?
_____

3 When was it sent?
_____

4 Why was it a problem?
_____

5 How many e-mails does she get?
_____

6 Who sends them?
_____

7 At what time does she check her messages?
_____

8 Whose problem is it?
_____

My score on this activity: _____ / 8
Do I need more practice? (circle one)   Yes   No

Express Yourself Activity Book | Review 2

Name: _____ Group: _____ Date: _____

2 Present Progressive: A Week in the Forest

Last summer, I spent a week in the forest with my uncle, who is a camp instructor. This is the first day of our outdoor expedition.

> Describe what the characters in the illustration are doing by changing the infinitive verb to the present progressive tense.

1. The girls (to start) _____ a fire.
2. The boys (to sleep) _____ in the tent.
3. The camp instructor (to read) _____ a map.
4. The squirrel (to eat) _____ a nut.
5. The dog (to drink) _____ water.

My score on this activity: _____ / 5
Do I need more practice? (circle one)   Yes   No

3 Past Progressive, Simple Present, Simple Past and Future: A Week in the Forest

Now that you have described the scene above, try changing the verb tenses. Make sure your sentences in Activity 2 are correct before you do this next activity.

> Choose three of your present progressive sentences and rewrite them using the verb tenses below.

Example: I am **looking** at the beautiful landscape.

Past Progressive:	I was looking at the beautiful landscape.
Present:	I look at the beautiful landscape.
Past:	I looked at the beautiful landscape.
Future:	I will look at the beautiful landscape.

Review 2 | Activity Book

Name: _____ Group: _____ Date: _____

1 Past Progressive: _____
Present: _____
Past: _____
Future: _____

2 Past Progressive: _____
Present: _____
Past: _____
Future: _____

3 Past Progressive: _____
Present: _____
Past: _____
Future: _____

My score on this activity: _____ / 12
Do I need more practice? (circle one)   Yes   No

4 Modals: A Great Idea

Sophie and Jesper are two students who want to change their school with a small act of kindness toward the planet.

› Fill in this conversation between Sophie and Jesper.
› Use the appropriate modal auxiliary from the Word Bank below.

Word Bank: Could   can   will   have to   should

Jesper: We _____ come up with an idea for a project.

Sophie: I had an idea after working on Unit 3 in this book. We _____ start a recycling program at school. We waste so much paper every day.

Jesper: That's a great idea, but we _____ talk to the English teacher before we do anything. She _____ give us ideas on how to present the plan to the principal.

Sophie: At what time _____ you meet me tomorrow?

Jesper: I _____ meet you after lunch.

Sophie: Great! See you then!

My score on this activity: _____ / 5
Do I need more practice? (circle one)   Yes   No

Express Yourself Activity Book | Review 2

Name: _____ Group: _____ Date: _____

5 Prepositions: A Visitor's E-mail

Charles, a friend I met when we went to Toronto on a school trip this year, came to visit me last weekend. He sent me an e-mail with a few questions the night before his arrival. He seemed a bit nervous about taking the bus.

> Use prepositions from the Word Bank to answer Charles' questions.

Word Bank:

at	from	in	in front of
inside	near	on	outside

1. **Q:** When will you pick me up?
   A: _____ 7:30 tomorrow night.
2. **Q:** Where will we meet?
   A: _____ the bus terminal.
3. **Q:** Where is the terminal exactly?
   A: _____ the park.
4. **Q:** Where will you be waiting?
   A: I will be waiting _____ the terminal.
5. **Q:** Will you have your cell phone?
   A: Yes, I always keep it _____ my jacket.
6. **Q:** If there is a big crowd there, how will you find me?
   A: Don't worry, I will look for you _____ the exit.

My score on this activity: _____ / 6
Do I need more practice? (circle one)   Yes   No

6 Pronouns and Possessive Adjectives: A Movie Review

> Read this movie review.
> Circle all the pronouns and possessive adjectives. The first one has been done for you.

Sunshine Girl is one of (my) favourite movies. It is the story of a family determined to get their young daughter into a beauty contest. Their family is just like mine! One of the funny parts of the movie is when the girl practices her dance routine with her grandfather. They take themselves so seriously! The nicest part is when the main character's brother tells the girl he loves her. Sunshine Girl delivers its message simply and beautifully. I recommend that you see it.

My score on this activity: _____ / 12
Do I need more practice? (circle one)   Yes   No

Name: _____ Group: _____ Date: _____

7 Articles: A Great Job

› Underline all the articles in this text.

My aunt is a waitress at the Queen Elizabeth Hotel, which is a fancy hotel in Montréal. The way she talks about her job makes me want to work there! She likes the people she works with. She never works during the day. She has a great meal every time she works—she made me try an apple strudel last time I visited her there, and it was delicious! She meets a lot of famous people. She serves fifty people a night and her salary is great!

My score on this activity: _____ / 10
Do I need more practice? (circle one)   Yes   No

8 Comparatives and Superlatives: Which Game is Better?

Shona and Lee Ann are talking about their favourite video games.

› Write the comparative or superlative form of the word in parentheses.
› Use the context of each sentence to decide which form to write.

1. Shona: I think that adventure games are really the _____ games of all. (good)

2. Lee Ann: I don't agree. I really think that strategy games are _____ adventure games. (good)

3. Shona: Why do you think that they are _____ games? (cool)

4. Lee Ann: Because strategy games are _____ (intelligent) adventure games and they are _____. (exciting)

5. Shona: Yes, but they are also _____ adventure games. (expensive)

6. Lee Ann: That's not always true: you can buy your games when they are on sale. Then they will be _____ the regular price. (cheap)

My score on this activity: _____ / 7
Do I need more practice? (circle one)   Yes   No

Express Yourself Activity Book | Review 2

Name: _____ Group: _____ Date: _____

Self-Evaluation

> First, calculate your score for the activities you completed.

1 _____ / 8   **4** _____ / 5   **7** _____ / 10

2 _____ / 5   **5** _____ / 6   **8** _____ / 7

3 _____ / 12   **6** _____ / 12

My total score: _____ / 65 = _____ %

> Then answer these questions to evaluate what you've learned.
> Check all the responses that apply to you.

1 What Smart Structure are you good at?
- ☐ Questions, Simple Present
- ☐ Simple Past
- ☐ Pronouns
- ☐ Articles
- ☐ Modals and Conditional Form
- ☐ Present Progressive
- ☐ Comparatives and Superlatives
- ☐ Prepositions
- ☐ Past Progressive
- ☐ Future

2 What Smart Structure do you still need to review?
- ☐ Questions, Simple Present
- ☐ Simple Past
- ☐ Pronouns
- ☐ Articles
- ☐ Modals and Conditional Form
- ☐ Present Progressive
- ☐ Comparatives and Superlatives
- ☐ Prepositions
- ☐ Past Progressive
- ☐ Future

3 How will you review these Smart Structures now? (Check all that apply.)
- ☐ I will go back and look at the rules again in the Student Book.
- ☐ I will ask my teacher or someone else for help explaining the rules to me.
- ☐ I will do some more exercises to practice.

Name: _____   Group: _____   Date: _____

Irregular Verbs

Tips to Help You Remember

1. Read the irregular verbs out loud in the simple past.
2. Write them down.
3. Use them in sentences.
4. Practise them with a friend.
5. Learn five new irregular verbs each week.

List of Irregular Verbs

Base Form	Simple Past	Meaning
1 awake	awoke	
2 be	was, were	
3 beat	beat	
4 become	became	
5 begin	began	
6 bend	bent	
7 bet	bet	
8 bid	bid	
9 bite	bit	
10 bleed	bled	
11 blow	blew	
12 break	broke	
13 bring	brought	
14 build	built	
15 burn	burnt	
16 buy	bought	
17 catch	caught	
18 choose	chose	
19 come	came	
20 cost	cost	
21 cut	cut	
22 deal	dealt	
23 dive	dove	
24 do	did	
25 draw	drew	

Base Form	Simple Past	Meaning
26 drink	drank	
27 drive	drove	
28 eat	ate	
29 fall	fell	
30 feed	fed	
31 feel	felt	
32 fight	fought	
33 find	found	
34 fly	flew	
35 forbid	forbade	
36 forget	forgot	
37 forgive	forgave	
38 freeze	froze	
39 get	got	
40 give	gave	
41 go	went	
42 grow	grew	
43 hang	hung	
44 have	had	
45 hear	heard	
46 hide	hid	
47 hit	hit	
48 hold	held	
49 hurt	hurt	
50 keep	kept	

Express Yourself Activity Book | Irregular Verbs

Base Form	Simple Past	Meaning
51 know	knew	
52 lead	led	
53 leave	left	
54 let	let	
55 lie	lay	
56 lose	lost	
57 make	made	
58 mean	meant	
59 meet	met	
60 pay	paid	
61 put	put	
62 read	read	
63 ride	rode	
64 ring	rang	
65 run	ran	
66 say	said	
67 see	saw	
68 sell	sold	
69 send	sent	
70 set	set	
71 shake	shook	
72 shoot	shot	
73 shut	shut	

Base Form	Simple Past	Meaning
74 sing	sang	
75 sit	sat	
76 sleep	slept	
77 speak	spoke	
78 spend	spent	
79 split	split	
80 spread	spread	
81 stand	stood	
82 steal	stole	
83 stick	stuck	
84 sting	stung	
85 stink	stank	
86 swear	swore	
87 sweep	swept	
88 swim	swam	
89 take	took	
90 teach	taught	
91 tell	told	
92 think	thought	
93 throw	threw	
94 understand	understood	
95 win	won	
96 write	wrote	

Irregular Verbs | Activity Book